Praise for

RECLAIM YOUR NERVOUS SYSTEM

"In Reclaim Your Nervous System, *Mastin Kipp skillfully unravels and demystifies the profound experiences associated with trauma, providing survivors with optimism and empowerment. Through a relatable narrative, Kipp seamlessly blends practical therapeutic techniques with the wisdom acquired through his own journey and his interactions with clients. The result is a practical framework that effectively separates the embodied experience of trauma from specific events and diagnostic labels, fostering positive outcomes for those on the path to healing."*

— **Dr. Stephen W. Porges, Ph.D.**, creator of the Polyvagal Theory

"Mastin Kipp has pioneered a science-backed and holistic road map to help you heal and create positive change, no matter what you've been through."

— **Mel Robbins**, *New York Times* best-selling author of *The 5 Second Rule* and *The High 5 Habit*

*"*Reclaim Your Nervous System *is one of the most holistic approaches to healing I have ever read. Mastin does a beautiful job of presenting scientific, life-changing information through a lens that is full of heart and humanity. Throughout the book, you feel like your hand is being held by an uncondi-tionally loving friend, someone who has been exactly where you are, someone who is walking right beside you on your journey to healing."*

— **LeAnn Rimes**, two-time Grammy–Award winning, multi-platinum singer and songwriter

"For anyone who has ever felt stuck in old patterns that lead to shame and guilt, Reclaim Your Nervous System *goes deeper than mere positivity training to reveal a practical trauma-informed approach to help you finally get unstuck, make peace with yourself, and take the first steps toward optimizing your life."*

— **Dr. Daniel G. Amen, M.D.**, physician, adult and child psychiatrist, and author of *Change Your Brain Every Day*

"Mastin Kipp has pioneered the field of trauma-informed coaching, and with this new book gives us a powerful, evidence-based holistic framework to resolve past traumas and create positive change so that we can sustainably upgrade our nervous system to be limitless."

— **Jim Kwik**, *New York Times* best-selling author of *Limitless*

"I think it's vital that entrepreneurs and high performers read this book, especially if you think you don't have trauma. Mastin Kipp has created a must-read manual for understanding how we work as human beings, how our past prevents us from growth, and how to apply the latest neuroscience to resolve our past and unlock our true potential for building amazing businesses that leave a lasting impact."

— **Dan Martell,** author of *Buy Back Your Time*

"Building upon the solid foundation established by the trauma-healing field, Mastin Kipp takes a pioneering leap forward, presenting a holistic, evidence-based pathway toward positive change and sustainable goal attainment. I urge therapists, trauma specialists, and attachment experts to embrace the road map delineated in this book, as it empowers your clients to make the leap beyond the healing journey of trauma recovery to creating a compelling future filled with post-traumatic growth."

— **Diane Poole Heller, Ph.D.,** author of *The Power of Attachment* and *Healing Your Attachment Wounds,* and creator of the Dynamic Attachment Patterning Experience Training programs, DARe

"Mastin Kipp has pioneered a path that helps us understand how to work with our nervous system and past traumas. By transcending our survival-based responses, he guides us toward creating lasting positive change, enabling us to heal the blocks that hinder us from creating true magic in our lives."

— **Colette Baron-Reid,** best-selling author, personal transformation thought leader, and business strategist

MASTIN KIPP'S

RECLAIM YOUR NERVOUS SYSTEM

ALSO BY MASTIN KIPP

Claim Your Power: A 40-Day Journey to
Dissolve the Hidden Trauma That's Kept You Stuck
and Finally Thrive in Your Life's Unique Purpose

Daily Love: Growing into Grace

All of the above are available at your local bookstore,
or may be ordered by visiting:

Hay House USA: www.hayhouse.com®
Hay House Australia: www.hayhouse.com.au
Hay House UK: www.hayhouse.co.uk
Hay House India: www.hayhouse.co.in

***

MASTIN KIPP'S
RECLAIM YOUR NERVOUS SYSTEM

A Guide to Positive Change, Mental Wellness, and Post-Traumatic Growth

HAY HOUSE LLC
Carlsbad, California • New York City
London • Sydney • New Delhi

Published in the United States by: Hay House LLC: www.hayhouse.com®
Published in Australia by: Hay House Australia Publishing Pty Ltd: www.hayhouse.com.au
Published in the United Kingdom by: Hay House UK Ltd: www.hayhouse.co.uk
Published in India by: Hay House Publishers (India) Pvt Ltd: www.hayhouse.co.in

Indexer: Shapiro Indexing Services
Cover design: Julie Davison
Interior design: Karim J. Garcia
Interior photo: Courtesy of Mastin Kipp

Cataloging-in-Publication Data is on file at the Library of Congress

Tradepaper ISBN: 978-1-4019-7915-7
E-book ISBN: 978-1-4019-6142-8
Audiobook ISBN: 978-1-4019-6143-5

10 9 8 7 6 5 4 3 2 1
1st edition, May 2024

Printed in the United States of America

This product uses responsibly sourced papers and/or recycled materials. For more information, see www.hayhouse.com.

To Magic, the best boy there ever was. Thank you for being my guide, for being my ventral tether, for being my glimmer, and showing me, through just being who you are, how to reclaim my own nervous system and find my joy again.

CONTENTS

FOREWORD

In a world that's ailing and struggling to heal from an array of traumas, both past and present, Mastin Kipp's new book, *Reclaim Your Nervous System,* brings clarity and light with a clear path forward to thrive beyond adversity. He makes a bold attempt to bridge two worlds that have been fragmented and divided for decades: coaching and psychotherapy. Many in the field of psychotherapy focus on the past and don't value what the coaching community brings to trauma-informed care. Many coaches, on the other hand, focus on setting goals and moving forward, and hold a legacy of inferiority when it comes to treating people who suffer from relational trauma.

In the world of social media today, there's an explosion of therapists, coaches, and influencers who are trying their best to meet the demands of people who are suffering from various forms of trauma. Who is qualified to treat those who have been violated by another? What are the regulations and guidelines when it comes to treating trauma? I can say that it is delicate work and requires a specialized skill set. Sitting with trauma and the level of vulnerability it activates in someone who has been violated comes with a risk of re-traumatization if done incorrectly. I've participated in many consultations with therapists and coaches alike where treatment has gone awry. I know therapists, with the appropriate degrees and licenses, who should not be treating clients who suffer from trauma; and I know coaches who have the skill set and knowledge base to safely navigate the treacherous waters of healing.

It's not the degrees they have or the titles they hold that makes one a good trauma specialist. It takes drive and determination. One needs to integrate theories and neuroscience knowledge with personal and clinical experience to be qualified to help someone else heal. One must be attentive to their own history and self-aware enough to know when it's okay to proceed and when it's time to seek supervision. Most of us are drawn to this field not only because it's interesting and we want to help others but because we've had personal experiences with trauma—either through a loved one or in our own lives.

It's clear that Mastin has done his homework. He's read the studies, explored the models, sought out consultation, worked one-on-one with clients, and has done personal work. He is a change agent, which can feel empowering in one moment and terrifying in another. I know it's been lonely for him at times working as a coach with clients who have suffered from trauma in a sea of therapists and ivory-tower academics.

Reclaiming Your Nervous System is a bold attempt and a big step forward, providing a clear map for helping therapists, coaches, and healers assist those who are carrying hurt and pain from the experiences they've gone through in life. Mastin describes the importance of moving toward the responses and reactivity associated with trauma as opposed to suppressing, denying, or exiling it. He talks about the value of a parts-oriented approach, which taps into the brain's capacity for state change, helping clients separate who they are from what happened to them. Knowing that splintering off into parts is an essential survival strategy during the trauma, Mastin describes harnessing the capacity for compartmentalization as a tool for helping individuals navigate their way through the healing process. He talks about the value of going back and revisiting the trauma, as opposed to approaches that support cognitive override or rely on top-down strategies that suppress emotional expression.

Mastin also shares personal stories about his healing journey, which demonstrates the importance of doing your own work in order to assist another in their healing process. We can't help others get beyond their trauma if we're unwilling to go to those places ourselves. I believe that this is one of the most important qualities in assessing the capacity of a healer—the interest and desire to look inward and do their own work in the service of helping others.

Reclaim Your Nervous System not only helps us understand the importance of looking back and being curious about the past but it also helps us explore the fears and challenges of moving forward into the future. Mastin states that both are necessary, in addition to our capacity to be present with the overwhelming feelings that were a result of the injury. He states that moving forward can be as challenging as going backward and offers a new approach that incorporates both. He talks about confounding factors that must be considered when dealing with complex PTSD such as cultural, gender-based, socioeconomic, and racial inequities along with transgenerational injuries.

The model Mastin puts forth, Functional Life Coaching, is a path forward that is holistic and neuroscience-informed, includes looking back, states the importance of being present, and describes how to move ahead with clarity and alignment. It talks about working with distorted beliefs while monitoring our clients' allostatic load, helping them expand their capacity to tolerate distress and release what no longer serves them. It's based in the key principles of Polyvagal Theory, showing the importance of coregulation (emotionally, somatically, mentally, and socially) while focusing on the corrective emotional experience, a key component to releasing trauma. It also talks about redecision, leveraging one's purpose, and congruence as important components of the transformational process.

Mastin, who has at times felt like an outsider both personally and professionally, has written a book that incorporates the theories of thought leaders from the past, includes neuroscience knowledge and trauma-centered models in the present day, and offers hope on how to move forward, paving the way for trauma survivors to live an aligned, purpose-driven life.

Who knows? Maybe 20 years from now, the next generation of healers will be referencing Mastin Kipp's *Reclaiming Your Nervous System* as they take on the charge of expanding the capacity to bring more trauma healing to the world.

With love and gratitude,
Frank G. Anderson, M.D.,
co-author of the *Internal Family Systems Skills Training Manual*
and author of *Transcending Trauma* and *To Be Loved*

INVOCATION

A day will come when you will be stirred by unexpected events. A part of you will die, and you will begin to search for the elixir that will bring this part of you back to life. You will seek the elixir in friends, lovers, enemies, books, religions, foreign countries, heroes' songs, rituals, and jobs, but no matter where you look the treasure will evade you. All will seem lost, and you will lose all hope that this magic potion even exists. This will be the darkest of nights, and the promise of certain death will lead you to the abyss of despair. But staring into the abyss, you will see the dim light of your own illuminated Soul. Your radiance will transform the abyss into the elusive elixir of life, and for the first time you will realize that all the while it was your own Light that you've been searching for.

READ THIS FIRST

"One does not become enlightened by imagining
figures of light, but by making the darkness conscious."

— CARL JUNG

Here's something fascinating I've noticed in 20,000 hours of coaching clients and hundreds of thousands more on my own personal development journey: we human beings may be able to send rovers to Mars, but we struggle to sit with ourselves. It seems to me like we should have solved this problem already; we certainly have every tool we could ever need. And yet we're all asking ourselves the same question: *How do I love myself?*

In trying to answer this question, I bet you, like me, have been working on yourself with coaching, therapy, energy healing, biohacking, psychedelics, meditation, seminars, and books. You've collected enough PDFs for life, but you *still feel stuck*. You wonder how it's possible to have done all that work but still find yourself in the same old patterns. Cue the self-judgment, blame, shame, and guilt. But let me begin with this truth: *It's not your fault.*

The answer lies in your nervous system. It's your nervous system that is replaying what happened to you, keeping you stuck, and making it seemingly impossible to level up in your life. The nervous system is one of the strongest motivators for human behavior, influencing everything you feel, think, and do. Your nervous system can drive you to create your fullest life—and it can keep you from moving forward.

I've worked with thousands of clients in exactly this scenario. I train therapists, psychiatrists, and psychotherapists. I don't have any certifications or degrees, but I can go toe-to-toe with the best researchers and practitioners in neuroscience to push the field forward with healthy debate. What I *do* have is an extensive knowledge base; I'm a walking encyclopedia with 20,000 hours of practice using that knowledge to help people improve their lives. I love academia, and I also recognize there's an important difference between what I do and what researchers in the halls of academia do: if my tactics don't work, I go out of business. In all my coaching, I'm focused on helping clients create positive change.

If you're like the incredible, courageous individuals I've worked with over the years, these assumptions will feel familiar:

- You might think if you're doing this work, you shouldn't be getting triggered or experiencing emotional blocks.

- Your goal in this work is to amplify your positive emotions, and you'd like to avoid the negative ones as much as possible.

What if I told you that by chasing these goals, you've been avoiding some of the most important data for your development? What if I told you your triggers, emotional blocks, and resistance to negative emotions are the gateways to your next level?

Maybe you'd rather throw this book out a window than believe those ideas. After all, there are coaches who focus on helping people feel their positive emotions, like Dr. Joe Dispenza with his quantum healing work, or Tony Robbins asserting that if you change your story, you can change your state. These are beautiful approaches. But if the work you're doing is not trauma-informed, you risk bypassing the parts of you—like your frustration, avoidance, and grief—that contain the deepest wisdom for your healing and growth.

The modalities you've tried can be wonderful tools, but if they haven't been working, it might be a sign that deeper healing is needed before those tools can be effective. The CrossFit trainers at your gym don't need to be physical therapists to help you get fit, but if you walk into a CrossFit class with a broken ankle, the workout isn't going to help you heal. You need to heal the ankle first, and then you can get stronger again. Similarly, we can't bypass our negative emotions and experiences. Nor would we want to, because these emotions and triggers can be our greatest gifts and our wisest teachers.

The latest neuroscience suggests that you are stuck because there are specific emotions you are either avoiding or afraid of feeling.[1] It's not just you—all human beings avoid what hurts. However, what we fear isn't *life*; we fear our *emotions about life*. Turning off feelings makes sense in real emergencies. When your house is on fire, or you're fighting a battle, you need to be in a specific focused state to survive. But when the crisis is over and you continue to shut down the emotions you fear, what do you think happens to the part of you that feels that way? You've just told that part of you it's not welcome here. Think about what it feels like to be exiled. You become stuck in your business, your chronic health problems, and your relationship patterns, because you're leaving parts of yourself behind. If you don't include all of your emotions, you're writing off the most important information you could possibly have about how to reach the next level of your life.

So what emotions are you avoiding? Research says they fall into one of these seven categories:

- Anger, assertion, and stress
- Sadness, grief, and guilt
- Attachment and closeness
- Sexual feelings
- Positive feelings toward yourself
- Interest and excitement
- Enjoyment and joy[2]

Your anger could burn you. Your grief could drown you. Perhaps when you start to feel close to someone, you get scared of feeling vulnerable, so you shut down your attachment. Maybe you grew up in a religious community where sexual feelings were shunned. When have you not allowed yourself to feel that you were a good person who deserved good things, or to receive good things? When did you tone down your excitement about something because the people you were around didn't support your excitement? When did you shut down your joy because it didn't feel safe? Look through the list and take a guess at which emotions you avoid. What would be possible in your life—in your health, your wealth, your relationships, your business—if this emotion didn't stop you in your tracks?

For me, the emotion I avoid most is grief. I have spent hundreds of thousands of dollars trying not to feel grief. I will try any practice to turn off this emotion. I will go on a cleanse, sit in an ice bath, and drink green juice for days. I will do somatic work, breath work, energy work. Just don't make me feel grief. Meanwhile, my avoidance will limit the effectiveness of any practice or modality I try.

If you could regulate the one emotion you've been working so hard to suppress, your whole life would change. Take a moment to identify: What do you want to feel, and what do you want to avoid? Perhaps you're thinking, *I want to feel joy, but don't let me get angry.* But don't you think that to do things that are joyful you might have to bump into some frustration and anger? Or maybe you want to feel close to someone but not feel grief. But if you've lost anyone or anything in your life that was important to you, you know it's impossible to be close to someone and not have grief arise at some point. Within the emotion you're avoiding is a master lesson in your life, because that emotion will point you to the cause: something happened when you were younger that taught you that feeling is not safe.

To move forward, you have to help your nervous system feel safe enough to experience and release the specific emotions you've been suppressing. Avoiding a relationship with these emotions is like avoiding an injury. When you break your ankle, you might need surgery and you might need to heal, but then it's time to get stronger with physical therapy and training. Eventually, the work progresses from strengthening to performance, and then from performance to optimization. The constant throughout each of these stages is that you need to build capacity to level up. When it comes to inner work, the key is to learn how to self-regulate and create greater nervous system capacity to experience all your emotions.

What would be possible if you were okay, no matter how you felt? Another way to ask that question is: What would be possible for you if you could experience all of your emotions without becoming dysregulated and getting bumped off track? What you'll discover throughout this book is that it's possible to heal—and it's possible to go beyond healing to build capacity. As you move forward, you're going to experience dysregulation, but it's possible to return to regulation as you grow skilled with experiencing uncomfortable feelings.

The bigger the dreams, the bigger your purpose must be to bring them to life. A nervous system that has more capacity to self-regulate can take on more challenges. No matter what your background is, self-regulation is the key to unlocking your true potential.

When I started on my own healing journey, no one prepared me with the knowledge that there would be an emotion or two that would show up along the way and take me out. It took me investing lots of money in my own personal development to realize that whether we go on a therapy journey, a coaching journey, or a spiritual journey, there is a Pandora's box of emotions lying in wait. We try to set goals, grow businesses, be successful—*but dang it, why is grief still here? Why am I having a hard time with anger? Why can't I let positive emotions about myself be in my system—and thereby, the money might also stay?*

Nobody gave me a heads-up that the journey would feel that way. This book exists to help you understand how the healing journey works, what it feels like, and how we move beyond healing into greater capacity. You'll learn what trauma really is and how it gets trapped in our bodies, and that we all have parts of ourselves that are still stuck back in time, at the moment and age when the trauma occurred. You'll have a broader perspective on how your environment plays a massive role in your health and well-being. You'll discover that you can't talk about trauma without addressing the systems that create most of the trauma in the world. You'll recognize that a big part of the healing journey is to go back and rescue those younger parts of yourself and let them know that you're older, wiser, and stronger than you were before. By learning to sit with the emotions you avoided and befriend the parts of you that feel that way, you can increase your capacity and your tolerance for uncertainty. The goal is to make it safe enough to be unsafe and say yes to new adventures.

When I got into coaching, I focused on performance; my goal was to help people achieve results. But I quickly learned there was often an incongruence between what people said they wanted and what they did. As I became curious about *why* my clients couldn't put their dreams into action, I started to realize they'd all been through experiences that had been hurtful; they'd experienced trauma, and it prevented them from continuing forward. As a coach, I'd been oriented from the beginning on helping people get stronger and grow their capacity, but I began to see the value in slowing down and acknowledging what had happened in my clients' lives.

Throughout our lives, we often give what we need most. Consider that I've done tens of thousands of hours of coaching—what does that say about how much coaching I need? When I slowed down, I started to ask *why* not just of my clients, but of myself: *Why do I have this blind spot? Why am I feeling this way? Why is this problem occurring over and over again?* It took time to develop the audacity and courage to admit that something had happened to me. At the time I wouldn't call it trauma, but something had caused me pain and held me back from expansion. I'd operated as a lone wolf for much of my career; where did I get the idea that I shouldn't have help?

Throughout the studies I read on the biology and neurobiology of trauma, researchers and practitioners placed a massive emphasis on acknowledging the wound, befriending the nervous system, and having an empathetic witness to whatever happened to the person working through the trauma.

In the world of coaching, the last thing you want to do is acknowledge that you are limited by what happened to you. But the irony is that in the acknowledgment of trauma or difficult experiences, we can create new possibilities. I began to wonder: *Why are coaches and performance-oriented people so scared to acknowledge what happened to them?* It seemed clear from the research and from my experience that acknowledgment would make them better, not worse. In addition, I started to learn about traumatized populations that didn't have the privilege I had. I learned about the high rates of abuse, particularly sexual abuse, that women had experienced. Before then, I hadn't known the privilege I'd enjoyed throughout my life; it made no sense to me that certain people couldn't just make up their minds and act on their goals. I realized not everyone experiences the world the way I do—in fact, most people don't. I don't know what it's like to *not* come from privilege and live in a white male body. While I'd previously focused my work with clients on building capacity, I became curious about what prevents people's nervous systems from being more flexible.

The trauma world is in some ways the opposite of the coaching world. The coaching world urges people to get stronger: *It doesn't matter what happened to you; you can create a new future.* The trauma-healing world implores people to stop overriding the past: *I see what happened to you. I believe you.* Once I delved deeper into somatic work, body work, and working on personal history, I noticed it was easy for many people to stay focused on what happened in the past. After all, most of us were gaslit about the hurt we experienced, or we spent much of our lives bypassing it. Learning to turn toward those experiences and witness them with compassion is an incredible skill.

Years ago, I led a seminar for practitioners about growing their businesses. Over the first few days of the seminar, we'd done somatic work, regressive work, and reprocessing to go back to their childhoods, uncover what happened, and discover the parts of themselves that wanted to move forward. On the last day of the seminar, we started creating plans for the future. The exercises had a strange effect on the room; everyone became extremely dysregulated. Though they'd had the strength and courage to revisit some of the worst parts of their lives in the previous days, as soon as we began looking to the future, they became visibly frustrated.

I stopped the seminar to ask them a question: "Who here would rather do more processing about your past than talk about the future?" Almost every hand went up.

Afterward, I talked to our team to understand why the practitioners had responded that way. The distinction that we came up with stuck with me forever: even though it's scary to go back and revisit trauma from the past, that's so much easier than stepping into an uncertain future where unpredictable things can happen. People already know what happened to them and how painful it was; they don't know what possible threats await when they step out into uncertainty.

The concepts in this book bring the worlds of coaching and trauma healing together. We can acknowledge the past, honor all our parts, *and* grow our capacity to perform better and optimize our lives. In my work today, I focus on leading from the healed part of my nervous system. I know as I move forward, my parts are going to speak up—especially the parts of me that felt neglected and angry—and I'm going to sit with them and listen to them. From their hurt I can reverse engineer the path out of the pain. As I move forward, I'm going to bring those parts along with me, because I know they're some of my best teachers.

As I'm sure you can tell by now, this book is not a quick fix for performance; too often we get so focused on finding a hack to improve performance that we miss the full spectrum of the experience of being who we are. Nor will I coddle you or help you compile an *Encyclopedia Britannica* on your past; I don't want you to miss out on your future. This book is also not therapy; it doesn't comply with HIPAA, nor is it based on the American Psychiatric Association's rules and regulations, or state licensure guidelines. This book doesn't contain medical advice or mental health diagnostics. This book describes what *works*, and it comes from the trenches of working with clients and building a business in which my survival was based on creating effective tools for them.

This book is about how to holistically love yourself: to make peace with the positive sides of your personality as well as the harmful or negative parts, and to understand that every part of you has a purpose. When you put the wisest part in charge of your life, you can create a better future. This is a guide on how your nervous system works, and how you can use that knowledge to understand your feelings, thoughts, body sensations, past, present, and future—and how to incorporate the tools and modalities you're already using to serve you better. That's what Functional Life Coaching™ is all about. My ultimate goal is to help you leverage science-backed and evidence-based methods to produce better results and enjoy your life.

What this book represents most is a love letter from my heart, soul, and purpose to the world. I want to give you everything I know about how to heal, move forward, live a beautiful life, and most important: love yourself.

PART I

THE PROBLEM WITH TRAUMA

CHAPTER 1

THE NEW SCIENCE OF MENTAL HEALTH

"Roads? Where we're going
we don't need roads."

— DOC BROWN

I was leading a seven-day trauma retreat in Florida when, right on the edge of a breakthrough, one of my clients became really upset. She'd been in and out of rehab centers for years, shunted from one psychiatrist to another, given many (often conflicting) diagnoses, and had come to the retreat convinced she was broken and unfixable. No matter where she went, she got the message that she just couldn't get it right.

I told her that made sense to me.

"Wait, what are you saying, Mastin? That I'm unfixable?"

"No. But when you're in a world of psychiatrists whose primary tool is a diagnosis from the *DSM-5*, it's so common for people to take on that diagnosis as an identity. A diagnosis is meant to be a label for symptom clusters—a tool for the diagnosing practitioner—but once a diagnosis becomes your identity, it's hard to escape that identity. But have you thought that maybe you don't have a disorder? That everything you've gone through makes sense and your 'diagnosis' could be seen as a response to what's happened to you?"

It was a group session, so we were in the middle of a crowd when I said this. I watched her face change from tension and shame to relief as tears welled in her eyes. She couldn't believe it—could it really be that easy? Seconds later, her relief quickly turned into anger.

"Why did no one tell me?"

For years, she'd carried this debilitating identity that there was something inherently wrong with her, and this identity had developed into shame. Now here I was, telling her that her symptoms could all be a response to legitimate painful experiences in her life, and the idea was so simple, so integral, she couldn't believe she'd spent so much time and money not knowing something so fundamental. Why did no one *tell* her? She was furious now—not with any individual psychiatrist but with the whole healthcare system, and she just wanted to throw the big, fat diagnostic book everyone always referred to right out the window.

Now, I don't diagnose people, but I believe in two things: (1) understanding where something comes from, and (2) always being prepared.

The first principle drove me to buy a copy of the *Diagnostic and Statistical Manual of Mental Disorders Fifth Edition (DSM-5)* for myself—the thick brick of a book everyone refers to when it comes to diagnosing mental health "disorders." I wanted to know what the diagnostic criteria were when it came to mental health disorders and understand the actual mechanisms of action of these diagnoses that my clients were wearing as identities.

The second principle is why I had the *DSM-5* with me on this retreat, along with 30 other reference books. You never know when you might need them.

I told my client she *could* throw the *DSM-5* out the window. I ran up to my hotel room, brought down the tome, and gave it to her. I don't think she knew what to do with it at first. Most personal development retreats don't encourage you to chuck a book, especially not the *DSM-5*; there is such clinical worship around it.

But her anger and body were speaking, so she threw it across the room, over and over, with the group cheering wildly, and I could see her body relax into relief and happiness with each throw.

All the healthcare providers who were supposed to be helping her had taken away her power. She was taking it back. Just because someone is a psychiatrist doesn't mean they're not going to hurt you, that there won't be some kind of lack of safety, or that their methods will work. The American healthcare system is neither a healthy nor a caring system. This doesn't mean the people who work inside the system are not healthy or caring; I've heard many doctors, psychiatrists, and healthcare workers express the frustration of being constrained by the primary agenda of the healthcare system, which unfortunately does not prioritize client outcomes over profit. So what exactly is this "system," and how did we get here?

IT'S (NOT) ALL IN YOUR HEAD

In 1921, U.S. president Warren G. Harding dedicated the Tomb of the Unknown Soldier, White Castle launched the first fast-food chain in America, and—the most important event for our purposes—J. N. Langley published *The Autonomic Nervous System.* Langley's seminal piece single-handedly introduced the concept of the "autonomic nervous system" (ANS) and established the ANS as a "brain-to-body" system that controls processes like breathing, heart rate, and digestion.[1] He is directly responsible for our mainstream understanding of mental health as a mostly brain-to-body phenomenon.

Today, when you read about most mental health conversations, there is a significant emphasis on the brain. So much so that practitioners have come to almost worship the brain as if it were the only place to look for insight. They've taken this beautiful and important organ, separated it from the rest of the body, and said, "HERE . . . look HERE."

Don't worry about everything else. It's all in your head.

Not only that, the mainstream mental health and personal growth models have boiled down our complex challenges and reduced them to two simple issues: chemical imbalances and limiting beliefs in your head (subtext: something is wrong with your brain and what you think). Combine brain worship with the chemical imbalance narrative and you get the basic thinking around today's mental health and personal growth protocols.

Brain worship has flooded over into personal development, where there is a major focus on "mindset" and resolving "limiting beliefs" as the keys to success. It has also spilled into the spiritual community, where platitudes like "change your thoughts, change your life" seem to be the key to spiritual awakening. It is the bedrock of Big Pharma, where a pill can change your brain chemistry and somehow make all your problems disappear.

The problem with brain worship is that in the beginning of the 20th century, Langley set us up with incomplete information. Langley missed something so important about the nervous system that when I mention what the latest neuroscience is showing us about how the nervous system really works, I get a confused look from most mainstream mental health practitioners, psychiatrists, and neuroscientists.

What did Langley miss?

Langley missed the entire human body.[2]

Look at yourself in the mirror. What's bigger, your body or your head? Imagine missing everything below your neck. Today's focus on the brain has turned most treatments for mental health, most personal development success secrets, and most spiritual insights into something reserved solely for a brain in a jar. But we are so much more than a brain. In fact, we've been guts longer than we've been brains. Our gut is full of mitochondria and bacteria that don't possess human DNA but are essential for our survival; we live in a symbiotic relationship with them. These mitochondria and bacteria have been around on the planet for much longer than our neocortex. In fact, our gut bacteria are the basis from which our nervous system evolved, while the neocortex is the youngest part of our nervous system.

Between our gut bacteria and our neocortex lies the rest of our nervous system, governed by reflexes and responses that became more complex throughout our evolution. Our dorsal-vagal system, which originally evolved in reptiles before we branched out of the evolutionary tree, creates our "freeze" and "retreat" responses. This system is approximately 500 million years old and governs *immobilization*. Next up is our sympathetic system, about 400 million years old, which creates the responses of "fight" and "flight" or *mobilization*. Our ventral system, the prosocial impulses that drive us to form connections with others, is 200 million years old; this system cues *relaxation*. *Then* comes our prefrontal cortex, the newest piece of our neuroanatomy, which drives logic and reasoning.

While these systems drive three primary states—immobilization, mobilization, and relaxation—they can also create blended states. What we experience as "freeze" comes in several varieties, which we see in post-traumatic stress disorder (PTSD). When a freeze state includes a state of stress, like a deer caught in headlights, your heart races and you feel scared, but you can't move. This is different from a state of dorsal immobilization, in which you have low heart rate and low energy; you feel hopeless, depressed, unhappy, and checked out—but you don't experience a lot of stress. Both these states are dissociative; the difference is that with sympathetic activation (as with the deer in the headlights), some part of the body thinks it's possible to run or fight. Pure immobilization sets in when the threat seems so large that it's life-threatening. Running and fleeing is no longer possible, and we start to dissociate. Put simply, evolution doesn't want us to be conscious while we're being eaten. New research from Dr. Ruth Lanius on the dorsal-vagal system's role in dissociation could start to explain why we are seeing different kinds of PTSD emerge, with some types eliciting more elements of dissociation than others. However, more research is needed to understand what mechanisms underlie these blended states.[3]

We'll take a closer look at each of these systems in later chapters, as we learn to work effectively with them. For now, the most important thing to know about the inner workings of the nervous system is that there's a hitch: *These systems respond in order of seniority.* If the lower or earlier-level systems react first, they hijack the rest of the system. Our latest nervous system updates are responsive when the conditions haven't already threatened our earlier mechanisms.

We've had more evolutionary time in our gut—and the rest of our nervous system levels—than we've had in our prefrontal cortex. Yet we idolize the brain, even though there is no way to improve mental health without first improving body-affect health. Think about it: even when you take a pill, it goes into the body first. We're worshiping something that isn't running the show— even though we think it is.

And because of Langley's focus on brain-to-body pathways, most research since then has concentrated on them.[4] We've been worshiping a false or incomplete idol since 1921. If the current state of our mental health and our understanding of the nervous system were a scene from a movie, it would be *Indiana Jones and the Raiders of the Lost Ark.* (Disclaimer: the following story is meant to illustrate a point about how important it is to have complete information when you go looking for something. The bad guys in *Raiders of the Lost Ark* happen to be Nazis. Let's set aside any need to make comparisons; looking in the wrong place doesn't make anyone a Nazi, and this example is in no way intended to be a commentary on mental health professionals. I'm referencing a movie I loved as a child to make a point that has nothing to do with Nazis and everything to do with making sure you have complete information.)

In the movie, the Nazis are digging for the Ark of the Covenant based on the information from one side of an ancient headpiece. They had to put the headpiece on the Staff of Ra at a certain time of day in the Well of Souls chamber, and the sun would rise and shine a light on a certain part of the city that would reveal the location of the ark. They had been digging and digging with no success. However, Indy and his friend Sallah are talking to a wise man, with a real headpiece that has two sides. The wise man says that the first side of the headpiece said the staff should be six kadam high (which was the height of the Nazis' staff), but the other side of the headpiece said that you would need to subtract one kadam to honor God. The Nazis' staff, without all the information, was too long. This leads Indy and Sallah to have a revelation about the Nazis' effort: "They're digging in the wrong place!"

The same thing could be said about today's mainstream approach to mental health, personal development, and spirituality. They are focused on the wrong place. The current approach has reduced your complex, beautiful, intelligent, and unified body-mind system down to some chemicals, thoughts, beliefs, and "disorders" that don't take your whole system into account, let alone the larger systems at play in our world that can have a massive impact on you (for example, race, religion, socioeconomic status, gender, and so on).

So, it turns out Langley only had one side of the headpiece. It had important information on it, but it was missing critical details to create a more complete picture. How much more complete and complex can the picture be? I like to think about the Langley-based model as similar to that of Newtonian physics. Newton's work was a revelation, but it was Einstein's theory of general relativity that totally changed the game in physics. When Einstein published his theory, it wasn't long before most physicists adopted $E=MC^2$ as the new norm.

The problem is that there is a plethora of game-changing data out there that's updating Langley's model, but it's not being adopted as quickly. Unlike scientists, Big Pharma has a financial incentive to keep the current brain worship/chemical imbalance model intact. And the state of our mental health today basically proves it. I mean, if it were just about fixing your broken brain or chemical imbalance with some pills, we wouldn't be where we are right now: the data shows that at least 50 percent of the people on antidepressants are still depressed.[5]

Langley did make some massive contributions to the field of neuroscience. But just like you need to update your software on your phone regularly, we need to update our understanding of how the nervous system actually works. We need to upgrade our approach to mental health, personal development, and spirituality from a brain worship (a.k.a. Newtonian) approach to the new science of mental health that is a whole body-mind-environment approach (a.k.a. Einsteinian).

When we understand the new science of mental health, we step into a hope-filled world that makes sense and normalizes "mental illness," decreases shame, and gives us answers to some important questions that humanity has been searching for.

A MENTAL HEALTH REVOLUTION

I love it when a book title gives you almost everything you need to know about the book. When it comes to the new science of mental health, perhaps the best book title is *The Body Keeps the Score*, by Dr. Bessel van der Kolk.[6] It has become the breakout bestseller that has put the topic of trauma on the map. Yet confusion still reigns about what trauma is, and therefore intentional and unintentional trauma denial persists, causing massive amounts of unneeded pain in the world.

Bessel is a psychiatrist and an M.D. He is steeped in the clinical data. He is truly a pioneer in the field of mental health and trauma, and he has spearheaded so many incredible evidence-based approaches like neurofeedback, EMDR, Polyvagal Theory, Internal Family Systems, and trauma-informed yoga. However, the hard part about clinical data is that it's difficult to transfer clinical data and insights into practical applications for day-to-day life. My intention with this book, in many ways, is to pick up where *The Body Keeps the Score* left off. I want the information in this book to be digestible, relatable, tangible, and applicable. One of my superpowers is the ability to translate clinical data and findings into simple-to-understand terms so that you can take action and implement all the amazing new insights from the mental health, trauma, and neuroscience fields.

While Bessel put trauma on the map, the research of Dr. Stephen Porges and the clinical work of Deb Dana, LCSW, have contributed in perhaps the most significant way to human development since either the Ten Commandments or the Sermon on the Mount. This power duo is responsible for discovering (Porges) and then codifying into best practices (Dana) the Polyvagal Theory (PVT). I've come to believe that PVT is the single most important discovery in the fields of mental health, healthcare, personal development, human development, and spiritual development of our time. It is a paradigm-shifting upgrade to our understanding of the autonomic nervous system that shapes our perspective of why we do what we do and why we get stuck.

Think of it as the science of safety and connection, a theory that gives you a new way to feel safe and live your best life. According to PVT, the human nervous system doesn't function binarily, in an on-and-off mode. Instead, our emotions and quality of life are influenced by our environment. Our mental health is a *response* to that environment and its varying degrees of safety, as opposed to something that is "wrong" with us.

Porges picks up where Langley left off and has helped us update the new science of mental health and the human nervous system—the first major upgrade to the field in over 100 years. In many ways, Langley viewed the autonomic nervous system as one-way, with signals traveling from the brain to the body. PVT updates that understanding to show that it is bidirectional. Eighty percent of the vagus nerves are afferent, meaning they move from body to brain; our body is sending clear signals to our brain about what's dangerous or safe.

I had a client once who couldn't move past her trauma or talk about it because her body didn't feel safe enough to explore it. She had experienced early sexual abuse and was tight in her pelvic girdle and on the right side of her neck. Whenever she tried to express her pain, her pelvic girdle and neck would tense, she would feel intensely sad, and she would stop speaking. Over years of therapy, she had developed this idea of herself as a complex PTSD diagnosis. But when I looked at her, I saw a person with a very ordinary response to deep trauma. We did a practice I developed called Kipp Heart Theory, in which we ask questions directly to the heart. When I asked her, "Heart, was it hard for you to be vulnerable?" the answer was an obvious yes. When I asked, "Heart, can I play with you more?" the answer was still yes. But when I asked the crucial question, "Heart, will you play with me more?" she felt an enormous surge of emotion, because the younger parts of her that were protecting her equated play with rape. She began to shut down. Instead of reacting to that emotion, I told her calmly that of course her emotion made sense. That response opened up space for her to decide what the affect meant. For once, her younger systems didn't have to fight so hard because they were finally being listened to and accepted.

There are a million ways to describe what happened in that moment. In Internal Family Systems (IFS), a therapeutic approach to treating parts of the psyche that hold trauma, IFS therapists would call this a process of "unblending." You could think of it as "depersonalization," where the trauma traveled from the limbic system to the prefrontal cortex. Or you could understand it as the system going from dorsal shutdown to a ventral-vagal response. All these descriptions, which come from different therapeutic modalities, are valid. But in the end, this moment mattered for this client because it normalized a terrible feeling. During a trauma response a person is reacting in the present to a situation that's nowhere near as bad as what happened to them in the past. *The reaction to the reaction is worse than the reaction itself.*

This is why it's so vital for a practitioner to create an environment of safety—and to befriend the parts of a person that feel in danger. Some people think they have "treatment-resistant depression," when actually they have "practitioner-resistant depression," because their practitioner does not feel safe to open up to.

This client cried after that release. She couldn't believe she was able to talk about it so quickly in a group session. She'd come close in individual therapy once or twice, but nothing like this. She asked for a tissue, and I gave her tons, which made her laugh-cry even harder—she had never had enough tissues before. I told her that her emotion was in the past: it was historical, not predictive. She could let go. She had spent years with counselors, but she self-reported that she made more progress in that 40-minute group session than in decades.

By speaking to her as a person and not a diagnosis, I destigmatized, de-shamed, and normalized her experience. I let the hurt parts of her speak up, stayed with them, and validated them. PVT shows us what is possible when we truly feel listened to and heard, and that play is powerful.

PVT ushers in a whole new paradigm for how to approach healing. And, while Dr. Porges has written thousands of pages about PVT, and Deb Dana has written multiple brilliant books about PVT, it's not catching on just yet. So, I'm going to do my best to bring you up to speed with the most important parts of this groundbreaking contribution. And we're going to start by taking a good look at what's wrong with our current mental health approach.

THE FOUR PRIMARY PROBLEMS IN MENTAL HEALTH APPROACHES

1. We're following an infectious disease model for mental health.

Right now, one of the main ways to treat mental health is with prescription medications. While there is certainly evidence for their efficacy, the data is clear that we shouldn't worship these drugs like we do today.

I still take prescription medication, but I've come to believe that it should be called prescription "supplementation." Medication is supposed to make something (like an infection) go away, whereas a supplement is something that supports you in a process of growth. Nobody takes a protein powder supplement and expects to get ripped on the powder alone; exercise is required. Prescription medication works the same way: it has some efficacy and can support your healing, but it's far from a magic bullet.

Take Prozac as an example. This antidepressant was approved by the FDA for use in 1987.[7] In an interesting correlation, depression has been on the rise in the United States since 1990, just three years after Prozac was approved for use by the FDA. In 1990, 4.07 percent of the U.S. population had depression, but by 2019 that number rose to 4.73 percent.[8] That may not seem like a lot, but that is a 15 percent increase in the total number of people with depression in 1990 versus 2019, meaning there are millions more people with depression now than there were in 1990.

The punch line: Prozac doesn't "kill" depression in the way an antibiotic kills bacteria. Thinking a pill can cure mental health—like it can cure an infectious disease—is the problem.

How would we feel about drugs that treat infectious disease if the numbers were the same? Let's take penicillin: discovered by Alexander Fleming in 1928, it revolutionized the treatment of infectious disease. In 1942, the first patient in the U.S. was treated with penicillin. In 1942, the death rate for tuberculosis was 43.1 per 100,000 people in the U.S., which is about 58,142 people.[9] Twenty years later, the death rate for tuberculosis was 28.6 per 100,000 people in the U.S., which is about 53,339 people.[10] That doesn't seem like a big change, but in 1942 there were 134.9 million people in the U.S. and in 1962 there were 186.5 million people in the U.S., so we made massive progress with a disease like tuberculosis, which as of 2018 has a death rate of just 2.8 per 100,000 people. However, if the data was the same as the numbers for Prozac, that would mean that in 1962 there would have been 78,492 tuberculosis deaths, a rate of approximately 42 deaths out of every 100,000 people, which is effectively the same as the 1942 death rate.

When it comes to prescription medication for mental health, what we've seen is small, incremental change—and that's all we can expect, because we're addressing symptoms, not root causes. One of the primary reasons why the numbers for prescription medication are nowhere near as dramatic as those for infectious disease is because infectious disease and mental health are two totally different problems. You don't just "catch" depression or anxiety or ADHD. These symptoms emerge within you over time, based on many different factors.

And while I believe that there is a massive future for psychedelics, which are currently growing in popularity to aid our mental well-being now and in the future, they won't work without a clear, integrated approach: they aren't magic bullets either. And when misused, they can cause really concerning side effects like psychosis and retraumatization.

Mental health challenges are chronic, ongoing, and based on so many more factors than just trying to rid our bodies of a disease that we caught. We are attempting to treat a chronic, inequitable problem with an infectious disease approach, which doesn't work. The data proves it.

2. We love brain worship and a top-down approach.

When you approach life change through the Langley-inspired lens, you are taking what's known as a "top-down" approach, meaning you are focused on a brain-based or mentalized perspective. A top-down approach includes modalities you may have heard of, like cognitive behavioral therapy, dialectical behavioral therapy, willpower, mindset, talk therapy, learning, affirmations, psychodynamic therapy, and neuro-linguistic programming, to name a few. Freudian therapy is a classic top-down approach. I would also suggest that while prescription medication is something that is ingested into the body, the focus is on the chemical imbalance in the brain, so I believe that prescription medication falls into the top-down approach too.

Brain worship is one of the major problems in our current treatments for mental health, and we haven't come close to focusing on and incorporating somatic and body-based approaches. That is slowly changing with Porges's PVT and other therapies. What's emerging at present is a more holistic approach to improving our mental health and well-being, one that picks up where Langley left off and challenges those who've put their faith firmly in brain worship to solving the mental health crisis. But it hasn't caught on as extensively as it should.

3. We ignore socioeconomic inequities and their impact on our mental health.

The third problem with our current approach is that we do not acknowledge, understand, or know how to manage the cultural, environmental, gender-based, religious, socioeconomic, or racial inequity or inequality and the impact of our wider systems on each individual population. Trauma is not created in isolation. We know that how we are raised and the quality of our attachment in early childhood has a direct impact on our mental health. We also know that in America, your zip code—and the economic, social, and environmental stressors that come with it—has a massive impact on your probable life outcomes. Look at the data from a recent study by Aetna: "In various cities across America, average life expectancies in certain communities are 20–30 years shorter than those mere miles away."[11]

This is staggering.

And it's not just location-based trauma. In 2008, white men and women in the U.S. with 16 years of education had far greater life expectancies than Black men and women with 12 years of education. White men live an average of 14.2 years longer than Black men, and white women live on average 10.3 years longer than Black women.[12]

Lesbian and bisexual women are more likely to suffer from chronic health issues than straight women.[13] LGBT adults of all ages have elevated suicide risks: suicidal thoughts, plans, and attempts are more common among this population.[14]

There are just so many types of trauma that it's ridiculous to imagine they don't impact our whole mind-body system. There is bullying, violence, complex trauma, intimate partner violence, childhood trauma, natural disasters, physical abuse, medical trauma, refugee trauma, terrorism, sex trafficking, sexual abuse, and traumatic grief. There is trauma based on race, religion, body color, and gender. There is cultural trauma that creates health disparities among minorities such as American Indians and African Americans.[15] These disparities endure across time and risk factors even when there are simultaneous advancements in medicine, thanks to the past and ongoing abuse inflicted by dominant groups on said minorities. Think mass incarceration, housing discrimination, police violence, the legacy of an oppressive past of slavery, and traumatic displacement of groups such as the American Indians and the resulting cultural loss. This in turn pushes these minorities into social disadvantages and stigma, which further widens the gap. Meanwhile, American Indians and Alaskans continue to die at higher rates than other Americans, and we pretend we don't know why.[16] How can a pill fix this?

The problem is that these stressors and inequity were built into the American system from its inception. Equality says we're equal; equity says we have the same resources. We can have equality and inequity at the same time. America has an inequality *and* an inequity gap, and this creates a disproportionate amount of stress on certain groups of people over others—and that stress needs to be released somehow. I'm not trying to say riots are appropriate, and I'm not agreeing with violence. But what else do you think is going to happen? As Martin Luther King Jr. said, "A riot is the language of the unheard."[17] It's simple neuroanatomy: you can only put someone in a dorsal immobilized state for so long before they go into a rage (sympathetic state).

All this inherent and systematic stress shifts onto the individual and affects their body-mind system. Any sustainable approach to mental health must be trauma-informed. As the Substance Abuse and Mental Health Services Administration states, our approach to mental health must "realize the widespread impact of trauma and understand potential paths for recovery, recognize the signs and symptoms of trauma in clients, family, staff, and others involved with the system, and respond by fully integrating knowledge about trauma into policies, procedures, and practices, and seek to actively resist traumatization."[18] We realize, we recognize, we respond, and we resist, in that order.

You can't call yourself trauma-informed and not acknowledge the systems that produce trauma. Yet we have been doing exactly that . . . for generations. The result is a mental health response that's not trauma-informed and can't fix the problems we face.

4. We don't have an aspirational model or vision to break the cycle of trauma.

These three foundational problems with our mental health approach culminate in the fourth fundamental issue: we don't know where we're going. Currently, we do not have an aspirational vision or model in place that clearly defines the path of healing trauma on a personal and systemic level that can help us break cycles of trauma permanently (on both the side of those who are abused and those who perpetrate abuse). And like the (sometimes) Good Book says, "Without vision the people perish." We need to create a new vision for breaking cycles of trauma for good.

To truly have a revolution in the treatment of mental health problems, we must radically change our approach to how we treat these problems, and we must place them into the proper context of each individual's environment. Our current approach to addressing mental health problems is akin to trying to turn wintertime into summertime by burning a really hot fire that lasts a day or so in the middle of January. Will that fire make it warmer? Sure . . . for a small period of time. But it will burn out and then we're back, stuck in the cold again.

WHERE WE'RE GOING

The rest of this book will guide you to not only learn about but also start to apply the most cutting-edge modalities to improve your mental and emotional health and well-being. We're going to pick up where Langley left off, and it's totally possible that by the end of this book your life will have changed—and you'll be more up to speed about these matters than many of the practitioners you know. Your understanding of trauma will expand, and this is vital, especially if you think you don't have "trauma," because you didn't experience "capital *T*" traumas like abuse, war-based PTSD, and so on.

It's time to update yourself and the industry as a whole. Langley's book was published more than 100 years ago, and we're older, wiser, and stronger than we were in 1921. Get ready for a paradigm shift and a whole new way of thinking about mental health and personal development. I'm reminded of the last scene of the movie *Back to the Future*, when Doc Brown hurriedly approaches Marty McFly to go back to the future, again. Marty, Doc, and Jennifer get into the DeLorean, and Doc backs up onto their residential street.

Marty says, "Hey, Doc. You'd better back up, we don't have enough road to get up to eighty-eight."

Doc turns to Marty and says, "Roads? Where we're going we don't need roads."

The DeLorean hovers in the air, pulls away, and then turns back toward the viewer. Just as it reaches us, it time jumps into the future as the iconic *Back to the Future* theme plays (I still get chills watching that).

And that's exactly what we're about to do, because where we're going, we don't need roads either.

CHAPTER 2

WHAT IS TRAUMA?

"Trauma is perhaps the most avoided,
ignored, belittled, denied, misunderstood,
and untreated cause of human suffering."

— PETER LEVINE, PH.D.

September 27, 2018, is a date that will live in infamy for the families of trauma survivors and practitioners. Like many Americans, that day I was glued to the television to watch Dr. Christine Blasey Ford, a professor and research psychologist at the Stanford University School of Medicine, testify before Congress in the hearings to confirm Brett Kavanaugh as a new Supreme Court Justice. On this day, the Senate did a massive disservice to the American people and the world. Not only did they misunderstand how traumatic memory works, but also members of the Senate actively tried to confuse the public about the nature of traumatic memory.

As we took in the hearings, many viewers saw the divide between Republicans and Democrats on full display. But this isn't about politics; this is about science. Senators from both parties seemed to agree that Dr. Ford had been attacked—shoved into a room by two men and pinned down on the bed—but senators who supported Kavanaugh attempted to poke holes in the accuracy of Dr. Ford's traumatic memory.

In her line of questioning, Senator Dianne Feinstein posed an important question to Dr. Ford. "I want to ask you one question about the attack itself," she said. "You were very clear about the attack. Being pushed into the room, you say you don't know quite by whom, but that it was Brett Kavanaugh that covered your mouth to prevent you from screaming, and then you escaped. How are you so sure that it was he?"

Dr. Ford clearly explained to Senator Feinstein: "The same way that I'm sure that I'm talking to you right now. Just basic memory functions and also just the level of norepinephrine and the epinephrine in the brain that, as you know, encodes that neurotransmitter, that codes memories into the hippocampus, and so the trauma-related experience is locked there, whereas other details kind of drift."

Senator Patrick Leahy asked which part of the near-rape had stuck in Dr. Ford's memory the most. And perhaps the single most important thing that Dr. Ford said in her testimony was: "Indelible in the hippocampus is the laughter. The uproarious laughter between the two, and their having fun at my expense."

That's the core of traumatic memory right there: Remembering with every detail of the moment, yet not being able to recall details from before those moments or after those moments with any sort of clarity.

Typically, prosecutors bring in expert witnesses to testify on specialized topics like traumatic memory. Did the Senate bring in Drs. Porges, Bessel van der Kolk, or Peter Levine to help us understand the credibility of Dr. Ford's statements? No. The expert who was brought in to question Dr. Ford was a lawyer from Arizona, Rachel Mitchell, who prosecuted sex crimes. So, while Ms. Mitchell wasn't an expert on how traumatic memory works, she did know enough about trauma to serve a different purpose. Ms. Mitchell asked Dr. Ford for specific details of what happened before and after the "indelible event"—knowing full well that the nature of traumatic memory is to vividly recall the moment of trauma, but not be able to do the same with events before and after the traumatic moment.

As I watched, it felt to me as if Dr. Ford's abuse was happening all over again. The hearing left me heartbroken and unable to find words for what I was feeling deep in my core.

A month later, on October 25, 2018, I received an e-mail reply from Dr. Stephen Porges, with whom I had shared my utter disgust with how Dr. Christine Blasey Ford was being treated during the Brett Kavanaugh confirmation hearings. The exact words I wrote in my e-mail to Dr. Porges were, "This whole Kavanaugh thing has me at a whole new level of 'hell no.'" You see, it was so obvious to me that what Dr. Ford was telling us was highly credible based on how traumatic memory actually works.

Dr. Porges replied, "You're right about the Kavanaugh experience," and included an invitation to join his newly started Traumatic Stress Research Consortium out of the Kinsey Institute at Indiana University. Attached to his e-mail was a letter he had written titled "Introduction to the Traumatic Stress Research Consortium." The three-page document distilled so clearly how I was feeling about the public's reaction to Dr. Ford's testimony. Dr. Porges wrote in this letter:

Although trauma affects all our lives, we, as a society, often don't listen to the voices of survivors. Instead, we bias our reactions on a pragmatic belief that traumatic events have only a transitory influence on both our mental and physical health. Society is often more callous, especially if the trauma doesn't result in physical injury. Where are the resources that are available to inform society of the profound impact of trauma? Where is the documentation on the consequences and post trauma trajectory of physical and mental health? Where is the information on the consequences on social behavior, on relationships, on intimacy and sexuality? Where does a survivor of trauma find the "road map" describing symptoms and a timeline of treatments that would lead to a more positive outcome? The Consortium is structuring a research program to fill these important gaps in our understanding of the experiences of survivors of trauma.

Though these powerful words, Dr. Porges made clear to me what I needed to do moving forward: *help the world understand what trauma is.*

At that moment, it dawned on me that this was going to be really, really hard. Not only are our systems set up to deny trauma, but if we can't understand how big dramatic "capital *T*" trauma works, how in the world will we understand how the less dramatic yet very real "lowercase *t*" trauma works?

Let's take a big leap forward right now to pin down what trauma actually *means.*

THE ONE TRUE DEFINITION OF TRAUMA

Spoiler alert: no one can agree on a single definition of trauma. A quick Google search will render all kinds of results when you try to uncover the essence of trauma. Here's a list of just a few different types of trauma:

- Developmental trauma
- Complex trauma
- Attachment trauma
- Medical trauma
- Grief trauma
- Identity trauma
- Disaster trauma
- Early childhood trauma
- Intimate partner trauma
- Acute trauma
- Interpersonal trauma
- Sexual assault
- Chronic abuse
- Bullying
- Physical violence

- Religious trauma
- Survival trauma
- Terrorism

With a list like that, it's easy to get lost and confused. To understand what trauma is, we need to examine the history of the word itself.

In Greek, the word *trauma* translates directly to "wound or damage." The Greeks used this word to describe mostly physical injuries. Terms like *blunt force trauma* come to mind in that context. However, as the study of psychology originated, became more refined over time, and finally adopted neuroscience, the definitions of trauma evolved along with the field. In a 1920 essay titled "Beyond the Pleasure Principle," Sigmund Freud wrote that trauma is "any excitations from the outside which are powerful enough to break through the protective shield."[1] This definition is easy to relate to physical trauma; the emphasis is placed on stimulus and events from the outside.

In his 1969 breakthrough book *Attachment and Loss*, Volume One, Dr. John Bowlby, the father of Attachment Theory, suggested that a traumatic experience could be "separation from mother, especially when a child is removed to a strange place with strange people."[2] As you can see, the concept of trauma changes significantly thanks to Bowlby's contribution. Modern definitions began to acknowledge that trauma wasn't just related to events and circumstances, but to the internal experience of stress and disconnection.

The Substance Abuse and Mental Health Services Administration (SAMHSA) defines *trauma* as "an event, series of events, or set of circumstances that is experienced by an individual as physically or emotionally harmful or life threatening and that has lasting adverse effects on the individual's functioning and mental, physical, social, emotional, or spiritual well-being."[3]

If we add in more recent definitions of trauma from cutting-edge research, we start to get a clearer picture. Dr. Bruce Perry defines *trauma* as "an experience, or pattern of experiences, that impairs the proper functioning of the person's stress-response system, making it more reactive or sensitive."[4] Dr. Stephen Porges takes a Bowlby-inspired approach to his definition of trauma: "Trauma is a chronic disruption of connectedness."[5] On June 27, 2019, at his annual Trauma Conference, Dr. Bessel van der Kolk described trauma as "an illness of not being alive in the present moment." Dr. Gabor Maté told Tim Ferriss in an interview that "the trauma is not what happens to you. The trauma is what happens inside of you. And, as a result of these traumatic events, what happens inside you is you get disconnected from your emotions, and you get disconnected from your body, and you have difficulty being in the present moment."[6]

As you can see, we do not yet have one clinical definition of trauma that we can all agree on, so, I made my own, which integrates and adds to some of the abovementioned ideas. I will share it with you here, in hopes that we can start to unite around a common definition of trauma for the rest of our time together:

"Trauma is any experience of threat, disconnection, isolation, or immobilization that chronically dysregulates the optimal health and function of one's brain, body, behavior, nervous system, immune system, endocrine system, fascial system, emotional body, or energy body."

— MASTIN KIPP, N.M.D. (NOT A MEDICAL DOCTOR)

Trauma is nuanced. It is less about an event and more about an outcome. If an event or series of events didn't result in any kind of traumatic outcome, it's hard to classify those events as traumatic. Why? Because, what's traumatic for one person may be thrilling for someone else (like jumping out of an airplane—if you want to traumatize me, let's do that). We must understand that trauma *has an effect on us*. That's why I define trauma as an experience or a verb that results in ongoing dysregulation of any part of our integrated body-mind system. This means to understand and heal trauma, we must take a more integrated and holistic approach.

THE SUM OF THE PARTS

Unfortunately, modern science is based on a reductionist model of understanding, where we attempt to dissect things to their smallest parts. While this can be valuable to understanding mechanisms of action (how things work), reductionist thinking alone does a great disservice to the *context* of mechanisms of actions. This is how we get into the whole "chemical imbalance" or "genetic" reasoning for mental health disorders. In reality, chemical imbalances in the brain and genetic factors in mental health can primarily be *outcomes*, not always just causes. How could a genetic factor be an outcome, you ask? A recent meta-analysis (meaning, a study of a large body of work) found that "emerging work has begun to identify epigenetic associations with traumatic exposures that persist beyond one generation."[7] What this essentially means is that emotional trauma that happens to one person can be passed down to their descendants. Trauma responses are inheritable. We call this "generational trauma."

What we are seeing clearly in the data is that mental health "disorders" aren't simply caused by "genetics" or a "chemical imbalance." They occur in response to many other layers of experiences that result in those outcomes. Factors like purpose in life, race, socioeconomic background, gender, sexual orientation, environmental toxins, and the quality of relationships must be taken into account to fully understand how chemical imbalances and genetic factors contribute to mental health.

We can't understand trauma if we try to look at the body as individual parts that have symptoms that need to be fixed. An impact on our body impacts our emotions. An impact on our emotions impacts our spirit. An impact on our brain can impact everything else. We must simultaneously take a reductionist approach to continue to understand the mechanisms of action inside the body and also take a larger, systems-wide, and holistic approach to understand what factors are causing these outcomes in the environment and over a life span.

YOUR SYMPTOMS ARE NOT A DISORDER

At this point you may be thinking you've had trauma, or you still might not be sure. Perhaps one of the best ways to start to ground these ideas in your life is to pause on the concept of trauma for a moment and examine the documented symptoms of trauma. Consider whether you've experienced any of the symptoms on this list:

- Anxiety
- Depression
- Post-traumatic stress disorder (PTSD)
- Insomnia
- Shame
- Guilt
- Anger
- Fear
- Hypervigilance
- Perfectionism
- Addiction
- Procrastination
- Inability to achieve or complete goals
- Lack of empathy
- Bullying
- Impaired capacity for self-protection
- Self-doubt
- Impostor syndrome
- Feeling worthless or ineffective

- Self-harm

- Suicidal ideation

- Lack of trust and reciprocity in relationships

- ADHD

- Chronic disorganization

- Oppositional defiant disorder

- Bipolar disorder

- Dissociative and personality disorders[8]

That's just a small sample of the effects trauma can have on us. If nothing on this list jumps out at you, consider the collective experience we all recently went through in the COVID-19 pandemic. Perhaps one of the most traumatizing things that can happen to mammals is to be forcibly immobilized or held down. That's why the lockdowns that swept across the world were so hard for so many people—because restraining people in this way creates a day-to-day traumatic experience.

Each person on the planet has had some version of trauma. But we don't need to debate about whether or not you've had trauma. Just focus on what's happening in your life right now. Are any of the symptoms above—or any symptoms you experience, period— stopping you from living your highest potential? If the answer is yes, then there is a high likelihood that there is trauma work for you to do. Because as you've seen by now, addressing only the symptom doesn't bring a solution. As Bessel van der Kolk writes in *The Body Keeps the Score*, "Prozac blunts the effects, but the experiences are still embedded in body and mind."[9] Prescription medication can make the work more tolerable, but it's not the work itself. Working with mental health is like working with chronic illness: the root cause needs to be addressed, as do our bodies' adaptations and the way we live our lives, especially if you've had more than one traumatic experience, as most of us have. And these traumas can manifest in many different ways to protect us and even create new ways of manifesting once we start to heal.

When you look in the *DSM-5*, every diagnosis has a symptom cluster. We name the symptoms, and then we blame the name, in what functional medicine physician Dr. Helen Messier once described on a retreat we co-led in 2021 as a "self-fulfilling feedback loop." As we saw with this book's opening story, the problem with defining a cluster of symptoms as a "disorder" is that people tend to take on a diagnosis as an identity. The goal of practitioners who wield the *DSM-5*—in addition to coaches, spiritual teachers, and therapists who aren't trauma-informed—is to define what's wrong with you. Therapy asks, "What's wrong with me?" and answers, "I have PTSD." Spirituality asks, "What's wrong with me?" and answers, "I have ego." Coaching asks, "What's wrong with me?" and answers, "I have limiting beliefs." All these approaches rely on the assumption that part of you is not welcome here, in this life, as you are.

But the adaptations your psychology has created to keep you safe make sense. Your ego makes sense in how it individuates you, and it's a necessary part of you, just like the rest of you. The limits of your beliefs make sense in the ways they have protected you. In fact, as Richard Schwartz and Frank Anderson say, "From the perspective of IFS trauma therapy, we believe that all parts have a positive intention."[10]

When I first started my coaching practice, I dove into the body and its mechanisms of action, which is when I discovered trauma. I noticed that everything I'd observed in my coaching was actually broken up into multiple modalities in the trauma field, which meant that I was practicing a combination of 10 to 15 trauma modalities that I didn't even know about. When I shared this with my friend Dr. Frank Anderson, he said this makes sense, because practitioners are working with the same nervous system. Internal Family Systems deals with the nervous system as other advanced therapeutic modalities like Sensorimotor Psychotherapy or multisensory processing—and I did too. We were seeing the same phenomenon at different ends of the spectrum. But using the word *trauma* openly was still taboo, especially in coaching. I remember talking to my marketing person, and he told me we couldn't use the word *trauma* to describe what I did. It was too big a word, too scary. It wasn't a good idea to talk about it. But Dr. Ford's testimony and the Brett Kavanaugh trial proved just how important it is to talk about trauma.

On August 12, 2018, I decided to come out of the "trauma" closet on Instagram with this post:

No matter what you've been told or diagnosed, know this: you are perfectly made.

There is a lot that the mainstream does not understand about mental health and chronic illness. We no longer live in an age of predominantly infectious disease, yet we are still treating people as if we are. Chronic illness is not a disorder.

A mental health diagnosis is not a disorder. What we thought of as a disorder, pathology, or diagnosis of what's "wrong" is such a limited view of what's happening.

I am not against any protocol that helps someone cope or feel better.

However, there is so much new science and data coming out that we must change the way we view both mental health and chronic illness. We must not only treat the symptom but we must go deeper into the root cause.

What is the root cause of most chronic illness? Chronic, low-grade physical trauma to the human body that produces too much of an inflammatory response.

What's the root cause of most mental health diagnoses? Not just the physical trauma, but also the unhealed and unresolved emotional trauma.

So, the body and the brain are doing the best they can to cope and operate in RESPONSE to the underlying trauma.

This is why it is insanity to only address the symptoms of chronic illness and mental health.

And we need to rename our diagnosis protocol.

Example: instead of Major Depressive Disorder, it should be called Major Depressive Response.

Multiple Personality Disorder should be called Multiple Personality Response.

Instead of Irritable Bowel Syndrome, it should be Irritable

Bowel Response.

Instead of Crohn's Disease, it should be Crohn's Response.

Instead of Hypothyroidism, it should be Hypothyroid Response.

Without taking the root cause of physical and emotional trauma into account when you are diagnosed, you are only being partially diagnosed without a full context or understanding of the underlying patterns that your body is doing its best to cope with.

What if chronic disease and mental illness symptoms were actually appropriate responses from the body to cope brilliantly with the underlying unhealed and unresolved physical and emotional trauma?

While I had held these beliefs for many years, and operated this way implicitly in my private practice, this was the first time I boldly stated what I believe to the world. And ever since that moment, my life has never been the same.

The response from people was overwhelming. The idea of focusing on a response versus a disorder was so revolutionary, I decided that from that moment forward I would make this theme a clear and explicit part of my mission to end trauma from now on. Since that moment, a wave of other practitioners and the general public have joined in changing the conversation about mental health. It's been inspiring to see my friend Nicole LePera, with her massive account, The Holistic Psychologist, pivot and begin to address a more trauma-informed approach, along with my colleague and fellow *Super Soul Sunday* peer Gabrielle Bernstein, who is acknowledging trauma more explicitly in her work. Now, there are waves of therapists, coaches, and what I like to call "Rebel Practitioners" who are centering a trauma-informed approach in their practice, and it's a total game changer for the world as this catches on.

It's important to understand the difference between the words *response* and *disorder.* The word *disorder* puts the onus on the individual, while the word *response* puts the onus on an event and the environment. I can't tell you how many people I've met who think that their diagnosis is their identity because they got a label from a well-meaning practitioner who was trained in looking for symptom clusters, not root causes, and who was stuck in Langley's brain worship model and totally missing the body and nervous system. An identity change can cause massive harm or healing. A recent study found that when an individual assumes the identity of their diagnosis, it "leads to an impoverished sense of self, low self-esteem and suicide risk."[11]

What I've noticed anecdotally in my clinical practice is that client outcomes improve drastically when the recontextualization of a *disorder* is reframed as a *response*. People exhale and blame seems to diminish. We are now beginning to understand that a large number of diagnoses in the *DSM-5* could very well be a sequelae (a secondary result) of trauma.

THE NATURAL DISTRESS OF DEVELOPMENT

As I briefly mentioned earlier, trauma can change genetic expression. We are just beginning to understand the impact that different traumatic experiences have as they are passed down from generation to generation. Recent studies do show that a parent's trauma affects their children.[12] However, perhaps some of the most compelling work that illustrates how we can become wounded so early on comes from the work of Dr. Beatrice Beebe. Dr. Beebe has conducted a significant amount of research on the mother-infant relationship, and how nonverbal communication like facial expressions and body language can influence how we develop. Believe it or not, we're starting to find that simply the faces your mother made when you were 0 to 12 months old could have a profound impact on how you are wired today.

What Dr. Beebe helped us understand is that, in many ways, the person who acts as a child's "mother" (which could be almost anyone) is known as the primary caregiver and is the main emotional regulator of a child's system in their first year. How attuned the mother is to that child will set that child up for how they are wired for life. This means that if your mother is prone to depression in your first year, it sets you up for a whole slew of possible mental health problems later in life. Dr. Beebe published a paper in 2018 that stated, "Infants with mothers who have difficulty responding appropriately to their mental states, as suggested by low appropriate mind-mindedness, may feel less known and recognized by their mothers, a key theme in the origins of disorganized attachment."[13]

Dr. Gabor Maté explains this phenomenon as well:

> *Most parents extend to their children some mixture of loving and hurtful behavior, of wise parenting and unskillful, clumsy parenting. The proportions vary from family to family, from parent to parent. Those ADD children whose needs for warm parental contact are most frustrated grow up to be adults with the most severe cases of ADD.*
>
> *Already at only a few months of age, an infant will register by facial expression his dejection at the mother's unconscious emotional withdrawal, despite the mother's continued physical presence. "[The infant] takes delight in Mommy's attention," writes Stanley Greenspan, "and knows when that source of delight is missing. If Mom becomes preoccupied or distracted while playing with the baby, sadness or dismay settles in on the little face."[14]*

We must start to understand that when we were young and vulnerable, the lack of attunement or the inconsistency of attunement was also a traumatic experience. If we are not safe (physically and emotionally), we develop survival responses to our environment to protect the vulnerable parts of ourselves.

Another important phenomenon to point out here is how a child adapts to the cues of their parents as they begin to make their own choices. Around 18 months of age, children start becoming aware that they are separate from their parents. This is most often experienced when children learn the word *no*. They are stating their own preferences outside of what their parents want them to do. This is a critical time of self-discovery and individuation for a child to explore their world and learn about their environment.

This process of discovery is called *self-activation*. Self-activation is the "capacity to identify and express unique and individual wishes and opinions, to act on our own behalf and to retain an independent sense of self."[15]

Another way a child self-activates is through emotional expression. It's powerful to understand how your early caregivers responded when you were emotionally dysregulated (angry, sad, defiant, and so on). Why? Because how they responded early on to these kinds of emotions had a profound impact on you, even up to today. You see, as we start to explore the world more, from 18 months to 3 years old, we rely on maternal emotional supply, support, and encouragement to feel safe in this big unknown and scary world. Without that emotional supply, we feel like we are cut off, abandoned, alone, and therefore vulnerable. Feeling totally alone or neglected at such a young age can be extremely traumatizing because our body knows we are vulnerable, and vulnerability at that age means we are easy prey for predators. This is why physical and emotional closeness are vital to us when we are so young. Without them, we feel like prey. So, if we get angry, sad, defiant, or express any uncomfortable emotions, and our caregivers withdraw, this creates a crisis for us. Why? Because we have a massive choice to make at that young age: Do I become myself and keep expressing myself and who I am (which is a psychological drive), or do I keep my caregivers close so I can be safe? We choose safety at that age, and we start to learn that the parts of ourselves that drive our caregivers away are dangerous, and so we suppress them. We learn that if we become our true selves, we will be abandoned.

This was discovered all the way back in 1972 when psychiatrist James F. Masterson wrote:

> *The basic conflict . . . is between a child's inherent developmental push for separation-individuation and the withdrawal of essential maternal supplies that this move entails. If he grows, his mother will cut off his supplies—but grow he must. Thus this tie that binds changes a normal developmental exercise into one so fraught with intense feelings of abandonment that the child experiences it as a real rendezvous with*

death. To defend against these feelings the child clings to the
mother, thus fails to develop through the stages of separation-
individuation, to autonomy.[16]

The words that jump out at me from this excerpt from Masterson are "rendezvous with death"—because that's what it feels like to the child. If we combine our understanding of how a lack of attunement and not allowing parts of our child to express and grow both create problems, we start to see the obvious origins of mental health "disorders." I believe it's highly likely that nearly every diagnosis in the *DSM-5* is simply a list of all the different ways a human being and their nervous system can become dysregulated. Every client I've ever worked with has a behavior that they want to change, and I can trace back from that behavior to a traumatic experience that informed their nervous system and shaped a necessary response.

As an example in my own life, my mother had a broken back before she was 20 from a horse riding accident. It became clear in her 20s that she had some major, lifelong problems to deal with, and the doctors told her it would be a bad idea to have children. My mother, being the person she is, decided to have me. After I was born, my mother spent many years in and out of hospitals and in bed at home suffering from intolerable back pain. Both my parents loved me. There was no abuse. They gave me everything, and I grew up privileged in many ways. But, because the focus was primarily on my mother when I was young, and because it was hard for my parents to navigate my dysregulated emotions, I experienced a lot of unintentional emotional neglect growing up.

I discovered a friend who would always be there for me, who would never leave me, and who always made me feel good. That friend was sugar—specifically, cinnamon and sugar. My father used to make me cinnamon toast when I was younger, and it became my best friend. Imagine my surprise many years later in my 20s when I couldn't figure out why I couldn't put down the Cinnabon roll (even though I had quit cocaine cold turkey). It was because sugar and cinnamon were linked in my body as love. To release those from my life would open me up to feeling all the abandonment I had felt when I was younger. You could call my problem Post-Traumatic Cinnabon Response. This insight, and link between sugar and abandonment, was far more helpful than anything else I had heard about "compulsive eating" or being a "sugar addict." It made sense why I was able to lose 50 pounds in about five weeks in Bali in 2016: I had my friends there with me, and I wasn't alone as I was working out and eating right.

Taking the approach that what ails us is not a disorder but an appropriate response to the underlying trauma is the next step in mental health, personal development, and spirituality. There is nothing wrong with you. Using the tools you had at the time, you've brilliantly adapted to your upbringing, your environment, and your trauma.

THE DARK PASSENGER

As we start to expand your understanding of trauma, it's important to add in one critical insight. While I believe that trauma is the root cause of many of our problems, including things like racism, bigotry, abuse, and sexual assault, I want to make it very clear that trauma is the *explanation* for these behaviors, not the excuse.

Larry Nassar, the disgraced USA Gymnastics doctor who was accused of assaulting over 250 young women and girls and was sentenced to jail for 60 years, most likely had trauma. It's highly likely that almost any perpetrator of abuse has trauma in their own history, but that does not excuse the behavior.

However, to truly change something, we must understand it. We understand that trauma is at the root of many of our social, political, and economic problems today. The more awareness that we can have around trauma's impact on us, our friends, our family, and the world, the better solutions we will seek out and the better outcomes we'll face.

Perhaps one of the best ways I've seen trauma described in modern pop culture is in the show *Dexter*. Dexter is a serial killer who lives by a code to kill only other serial killers, which makes him a killer but also a character we sympathize with. The big reveal about Dexter (spoiler alert) is that he saw his mother die when he was two years old, and this event was so traumatic that it turned him into a serial killer. This was a fundamental piece of his past that he could never change. Dexter describes the impact of trauma on him in a profound way: "I just know there's something dark in me and I hide it. I certainly don't talk about it, but it's there always: this Dark Passenger."

Trauma is a Dark Passenger in all of us. While you and I aren't serial killers, our own Dark Passengers can mess up our lives in other ways. What I saw back in 2018 while I was watching the Dr. Ford testimony was an attempt to hide the Dark Passenger of our times, which is trauma. But the pressure is too great. We cannot afford to hide or deny trauma anymore. And, just like anything that's in the dark, once we shine a light on it, understand it, and befriend it, we will come to find that the words of John 1:5 still ring true: "The light shines in the darkness, and the darkness can never extinguish it."

CHAPTER 3

WE NEED A HOLISTIC APPROACH TO COACHING, THERAPY, AND ENERGY HEALING

"Trauma is not just what happened to you; it's what is inside of you because of what happened to you."

— GABOR MATÉ, M.D.

The first time I really confronted the limitations of manifestation work was when I took on Jessica Mann as a client. Jessica is incredible: her testimony in the Harvey Weinstein trial secured his rape conviction and put him behind bars, creating a new case law on what it means to be a perpetrator in an imbalanced power dynamic. By the time she came to me, she'd been practicing manifestation for a while, but her trauma symptoms always eventually returned.

Jessica had been following the work of Dr. Joe Dispenza, and in her practice she would go into what Dispenza calls a "quantum state," which is a meditative state of "zero point" where you de-identify with your mind, body, and personality and simply exist as an unattached and unburdened entity. Thus, zero point becomes a place of limitless possibility, allowing you to train your body with new emotions. But Jessica was running into walls. And to understand why she wasn't getting what she wanted from this approach, we first need to understand what effect this strategy was creating inside her.

Dispenza's technique can be helpful in some contexts, but the problem with this approach is it makes parts of you feel unwelcome. All the "limiting" parts of you are transcended. This sends a signal to your system that some parts of you are "wrong." This, I realized, was a fundamental flaw in manifestation work that I'd begun to see across the coaching world: it's rooted in overriding parts of you.

Let's take another smaller example from Dispenza's work: when his clients describe struggles with depression, he urges them to find a feeling that's bigger than the depression. The idea of searching for a different feeling allows a client to structurally disassociate from the sadness and override it with joy or happiness. But when someone says, "Find a feeling bigger than the depression," they're asking the depression to disappear. The moment parts of you realize they're not welcome, bad things happen, because every part of you has a purpose.

The reasoning behind a state like depression, Dispenza advocates, is that "the body becomes addicted to guilt or any emotion the same way that it would get addicted to drugs."[1] I don't believe that claim. According to Dispenza, we get attached to the rush of chemicals in our brain when we feel sad or stressed, and then we end up conditioning our body over the years to be comfortable in that state. He believes the moment we can't control how we're feeling is a sign we're addicted. In this view, we have to transcend emotion to manifest our will in the world. Let's break that down. The American Psychological Association defines addiction as "a state of psychological or physical dependence (or both) on the use of alcohol and other drugs."[2] Merriam-Webster, on the other hand, defines addiction as "a compulsive, chronic, physiological or psychological need for a habit-forming substance, behavior, or activity having harmful physical, psychological, or social effects and typically causing well-defined symptoms (such as anxiety, irritability, tremors, or nausea) upon withdrawal or abstinence."[3] If we combine both these definitions, we're looking at a state of dependence with deeply harmful effects. To say we're addicted to emotions, then, is to say they're bad for us. And in many ways, that claim is true: intense and prolonged sadness that leads to depression, for example, can be harmful when it provokes suicidal ideation. But this approach ignores the *purpose* of these emotions. Every emotion has a positive intention. Calling ourselves "addicted" misinterprets the purpose of the feeling. We're ignoring what every emotion is trying to tell us.

This is why I don't use the terms *negative* or *positive* emotions: I call them comfortable and uncomfortable emotions to take the value judgment out of it. The parts of us that feel sad or stressed or competitive or judgmental—they are all here for a reason. Overriding them may work in the short term, but in the long term, you're not giving that shameful, sad, or judgmental part of you what it needs, which is attention, love, and understanding.

The same thing was happening to Jessica. She would enter these expansive states of joy and comfort, but then she would retract and her PTSD symptoms would return. There's a phenomenon called backlash when you push your nervous system too far—especially without a trauma-informed approach—and that backlash can be quite intense for people. When she finally came to me, I helped her understand that what she was experiencing was normal. The parts of her that were trying to get her attention were holding a wound or protecting her in some way. Each time she turned away from those parts, they held on to their wounds tighter. Together, we focused on turning toward them by practicing reprocessing.

The majority of healing modalities are teaching either bypassing or overriding emotions. This sends a signal that those parts of you are bad, unwelcome, and should be further suppressed. If you've ever been stuck trying to change your state and wondering why you can't, now you know. The good news is, there's a way forward that honors your past, anchors you in the present, and helps you move forward without bypassing or dismissing valuable emotions (especially the uncomfortable ones).

CARING FOR THE BODY THAT REMEMBERS

The American Psychological Association defines *regression* as "a return to a prior, lower state of cognitive, emotional, or behavioral functioning."[4] I would add a fourth category to those three: somatic functioning. Your body records the physical positions it was in when threats occurred, and those movements or positions develop associations with the traumatic event. A person who was raped, for example, and pushed face down on a surface, will experience a response from their body when they go back to that position, even if it's in an entirely different context.

Regression allows a person to go back into those trauma states—whether cognitive, behavioral, emotional, or somatic—and make a different choice, thus acting out a different outcome. They can revisit the past and put the pieces together in a different way to regain their power.

Regression with safety can be one component of healing, but regression without safety can be traumatizing. People regress, for example, around charismatic leaders; they move back into this childlike state where they're more willing to be compliant and follow rules, regardless of what those rules are, which is one of the ways cults are formed. This is why it is so important to do regression with safety, agency, choice, and consent—because if it's not done well, it can be retraumatizing.

The first step with Jessica was creating a space of safety and context. Only then, and with a lot of preparedness, did we go into positional regression. She was able to go into those positions of trauma and fight back, which was incredibly healing.

Turning away from the parts of you that are trying to communicate is unsustainable. No amount of joy you create from overriding can last. You have to pay attention and talk to them—now, in this moment.

Therapy looks to the past to heal. Coaching focuses on the future. The downside is that looking only at the past can get us stuck in trauma loops; looking only to the future pushes us into overriding our sadness. The missing ingredient is the present moment.

BEYOND TRAUMA LOOPS AND OVERRIDE

Trauma loops happen for various reasons. They happen when people revisit the site of the trauma but don't have any new context to integrate into it, which is why they relive the same event over and over. They happen when people are around the same individuals who traumatized them, without experiencing repair in those connections. Some people find it easier to talk about past trauma to avoid looking at trauma occurring in the present moment. Still others have created attachments around their trauma, and if they start to break out of the trauma loop, they become lonely and go right back in.

It's common for people to see a link between their past trauma and a present-day behavior they don't want. But they get stuck in a loop when they think of the past trauma as a cause: *I procrastinate because of my trauma, and the more I procrastinate, the more I reactivate my trauma.* One way to know you're in a trauma loop: you can't stop asking, "Why?" But as any weary parent of a toddler knows, if you ask the question why long enough, you'll eventually get to the answer, "because of the big bang." In the end, the answer doesn't help you move forward. Why did your trauma happen to you? Because of the big bang. The real question is: What are you going to do with it now to get out of the loop?

Trauma has a neurological basis. It's a multisensory phenomenon, which means it can be triggered by a sound, an image, a body position, an emotion, or context—and often all of these. This is why it can be so overwhelming. A lot of our trauma happens when we're young, when our body doesn't have the capacity to handle this multisensory experience in a meaningful way. But when we're older, we have a more developed nervous system, with a better-functioning hippocampus and prefrontal cortex. This means we now have the tools to engage with our multisensory trauma and piece it together in such a way that we experience it with more agency and control. This is our path to healing. But most people don't know this. So when their trauma is triggered, they experience it in the *same* way, without reconfiguring or changing the narrative. Over time, the more they experience the trauma, the more the neurons related to the trauma get reinforced. Neurons can trauma bond too.

Have you heard of the phrase "Neurons that fire together, wire together"? This is exactly what happens with trauma. Each time you encounter a trigger, your body is primed to go back into the trauma state, because that's how it's been wired. You have created a "paved highway" to the trauma state and a "dirt road" to regulation. The result is trauma loops.

Thanks to the work of Stephen Porges and Deb Dana, I've come to think of the nervous system as a ladder. The top of the ladder is the most advanced states and newest parts of your nervous system, which regulate healthy growth. Below that, on the next rung, is your fight-or-flight response. And then one rung below that is your freeze response. If you spend too much time on the second and third rungs of the ladder, you're essentially rehearsing stress. It reinforces the neural pathways, such that evoking and staying in that state of stress becomes second nature. What you practice is what you're creating wiring for over time. You want to build a nervous system that increases the frequency, intensity, and duration of good feelings, but to do that your body requires a degree of nervous system health. *You have to rewire your pathways to achieve that health.*

So many systems of healing don't take that into account. They introduce overrides that ignore the neurological basis of trauma loops and instead try to create states of happiness, without resolving the trauma itself. Neuro-linguistic programming (NLP) is a prime example. One of the core assumptions of NLP is that it doesn't matter what happened to you (i.e., what your trauma is); all that matters is changing your state now. People who practice NLP in this way try to override what happened to them; they try to move toward happier states by discounting their experiences. But that never works. It's a present- and future-looking modality that doesn't honor the value of the past.

Different modalities have different kinds of bypass built into them. In other words, they don't deal with the emotion itself; they circumvent it. There are four different kinds of bypass: somatic, mental, emotional, and spiritual. *Somatic* refers to your bodily sensations, *mental* to your thoughts and ways of thinking, *emotional* to your feelings, and *spiritual* to your sense of identity and self. There are certain situations where bypass is necessary. For example, athletes may bypass their emotions toward the end of a marathon or an intense game to complete it. Or someone caught in a natural disaster may need to bypass their mental panic, how their body is feeling, or their emotions in order to survive. But it isn't healthy to exist in this state all the time, because it means you aren't honoring your systems. Assume everything has a purpose: your sensations, thoughts, feelings, and identity. We've evolved to be more congruent, and if these parts exist, they have a function. Ignoring them is ignoring the wisdom they could teach you. Everything makes sense. If you haven't made sense of it yet, you haven't investigated it enough. You need a new approach.

My point is not to call out these modalities. Instead, I want to call *up*. A large part of why I'm writing this book is because it takes a long time for science to go mainstream, even after it is published. The aim is to present data, evidence-based research, and anecdotal observational data from my practice (that's not peer-reviewed yet) to help you take complex ideas about the nervous system, trauma, and healing, and apply them to your life. My core principle is this: Opinion doesn't matter. Research matters, and research is always changing. Personal truth does not scale to universal truth, and the only way to make progress is to be as objective as possible. I say this because it's easy to be swayed by charismatic leaders or experts—but just because they're convincing doesn't mean they're right. I'm not trying to pick on these established modalities; I'm trying to expand their work based on research so that we can improve the efficacy of our approaches. These systems have benefits, but they also fall short—and it's important to identify and talk about these shortfalls so we can all grow.

I understand I have my own bias and perspective, of course, which is why I'm publishing this book in the same way I would a paper—for you to dig into and rip apart and expand upon by approaching it with an open mind. That's the only way in which we as a field can grow: by having open conversations in public, by disagreeing and challenging, and by always searching for the research that makes us stronger.

THE FIRST PRINCIPLES OF HEALING

We're told we need to find the right modality for healing, but finding the right method isn't the most important aspect of healing. What really matters is understanding our relationship to the injury and our response to it. Every person has a unique history. No one is quite the same, which is why we need different things at different stages of the healing process. The first step to holistic healing is understanding its first principles, as opposed to deciding the best modality.

"First principles" is a concept from physics that refers to a basic proposition or assumption that cannot be deduced from any other proposition or assumption. They are the foundation on which you build all else. Elon Musk used the first-principles approach in understanding how to build a Tesla and SpaceX, because he realized that without abiding by the rules of physics, he wouldn't be successful. Similarly, there are basic first principles of healing that I've noticed. Look at trauma, for example. We know that trauma networks are created in our brain and nervous system based on experiences we've been through. We also know we can rewire those networks to create something new. One of the first principles of healing is *you don't heal a trauma network by overriding it*. The network exists. When we try to deny or push through it, we give it more power. Another first principle that I've discussed with Dr. Frank Anderson is that if you only stay in the trauma network, you don't really heal it. Within the trauma network, you're not creating a new future, you're just endlessly living in the old one. We can't be limited by our networks.

Over 20,000-plus hours of coaching, I've witnessed that many of my clients, when they first come to me, have been taught to use the majority of personal development, spiritual healing, and top-down approaches to violate the first principle of healing by trying to override the trauma. Similarly, a lot of therapy modalities violate the other first principle by focusing only on the past and not on creating new futures. It's not only about the past. So what then is it about? Our goal for healing trauma and moving forward should be to optimize your usefulness and purpose. There have been more studies on purpose in the last 5 years than there have been in the past 57 years, and the data is clear: purpose makes your life better. Search for "purpose in life" on PubMed, and you'll find over a thousand studies that prove it and much more.

A sense of purpose creates a different neural expectation in your system that primes you to find answers, which makes it more likely you'll find better outcomes. Purpose is the missing factor, and our goal in these modalities should be to optimize and increase your sense of direction. Uncertainty, on the other hand, or a lack of direction, or confusion about why things are happening to you leads to despair and depression. I know. I've been there.

STEPPING ONTO MY OWN PATH

I remember attending a screening party in New York City for the release of Oprah Winfrey's series *Belief* and spending the whole party chatting with Caroline Myss in a corner, ignoring everyone else. I was having an existential crisis; I didn't know what my purpose was or where I was going. But she told me, "Mastin, if you're not questioning your purpose at least once every decade, you're not growing."

Until she said that, I didn't know how much shame I was carrying about my lack of direction—because I was the guy who taught people about purpose, but I didn't know mine. And it took me back to the music industry and a life-changing event I experienced at 22. I entered the music industry at the bottom: I started as an intern at The Firm and then worked my way up until Fred Durst hired me to run his label Flawless at Geffen Records. I was over the moon; I was only 21 and was already experiencing so much success. But the president of the label didn't like me because I spoke truth to power and was a little too confident, so he got me fired by making up stories about me. And it crushed me. I'd put everything into that experience and now that it was ripped away, I didn't know who I was. I couldn't understand: *Why had this happened to me?* Years later, I found an answer to my question.

I hadn't even thought of trauma work or personal development when I was in the music industry: all I wanted was to be the next David Geffen (Scooter Braun would be the modern-day equivalent). But when I was kicked out, I started going to therapy and searching for answers. One of my clients in my management practice had a song in this movie called *What the Bleep Do We Know!?*, one of the first films about spirituality and consciousness. They were debuting the movie at a film festival at the Loews Santa Monica Beach Hotel, and I went along for the ride. I didn't fully understand the movie: I was both pulled toward it and weirded out by it. But on the way out from the movie theater, there was this cute girl taking Kirlian photographs that supposedly revealed your aura. I thought she was crazy, but she was cute, so I went to talk to her. Instead of giving me her phone number, she gave me the CD set of *Advanced Energy Anatomy* by Caroline Myss. It was a rejection, coupled with an "I think you're kinda fucked up and might need this book."

I let that CD set sit in my car for six months. But one day I began listening to it, and everything started changing for me after that. In her strict schoolmarm tone, Myss described how our choices fundamentally shape our lives. Our choices are our power. Once we become aware of the conscious and subconscious choices we make, we can develop a deeper understanding of ourselves and our priorities. So much of what Caroline Myss said made sense to me, and her work led me into Deepak Chopra, Wayne Dyer, and the whole spiritual world. But beautiful as I found that space, I also found it lacking. From a young age, I'd been taught to think for myself. My parents were scientists, and my father would always discuss the scientific method with me and how to form hypotheses. I entered the world empowered and always believing I can test things, which is why when someone makes a claim, I say, "prove it." Because that's how you know if it works or not. So even as I was reading all these spiritual models, I kept asking "why?" and "how does it work?" I didn't agree with all of it. And those questions led me to Bessel van der Kolk, Frank Anderson, Janina Fisher, all the trauma greats, and a more science-based approach.

It was only after getting into trauma work, helping people, going on Oprah's *Super Soul Sunday*, and gaining my own kind of following that I realized that the questions I was asking after my music industry career ended were being answered. I may not be able to exist in the industry as the next David Geffen, but this whole population of people I'd served before needed a different kind of service. The Me Too era brought that home: It became clear that there is a lot of trauma in entertainment, and the future of this industry is going to be trauma-informed. I could help these people—and I couldn't have if I *hadn't* been kicked out of the industry at 22 and found my own path back in. The dots connected, even though it seemed impossible they would.

This is not to say that the journey into what I do was easy. It wasn't a straightforward path: I discovered what I teach today by thinking deeply about what I see and noticing patterns across the work I do. It's a combination of intuition and my desire for proof. My intuition usually makes very good guesses, and then I step in and test to see if those guesses work. This process served me well across the years, especially as I tried to find my voice and what I wanted to say. Russell Bishop, the founder of the Insight Seminars, told me when I was just starting out: "Mastin, you don't need to be formally trained to help people. You just need to think your own thoughts and be honest about it." And so that's what I did. It wasn't easy—and I didn't know for ages how to *define* what we were doing, even though I knew our coaching was helping people.

I found the name and definition for what we do at a Mastermind called Consumer Health Summit, which is an invitation-only event for founders who are leading and redefining health and wellness hosted each year by my dear friend Michael Fishman. At this particular CHS, I had the honor of sitting next to the one and only Dr. Jeffrey Bland, who is the father of Functional Medicine. I've always admired Functional Medicine; it's about finding the root cause of the symptom of diseases (both chronic and acute). I realized the more I spoke with Dr. Bland that, with my business partner Jenna Hall, this is what we'd been doing all along: looking for the root causes of emotional blocks that hold us back in life. We were teaching a new method of coaching, Functional Life Coaching™. That's how our approach got its name.

Part of the approach of Functional Life Coaching™ is identifying first principles, so we can pinpoint the different root causes in our nervous system and in our whole body. In other words, what are the foundational things we know to be true about unleashing and creating potential and emotional healing? Think about building a spaceship: you need to have the basic principles of how flight works. You need lift, drag, propulsion. Without those things, you're not going to get off the ground. Similarly, we've mapped out a way of looking at an individual that we know works so that we can assess where they are with their trauma and their response to it. And once we know that, we bring in the different modalities that can help. Again, think of the spaceship analogy—now that we know what's going to get the ship off the ground, we need to actually build it, and for that, we need a door, a window, maybe a wing. We use modalities in the same way: as tools that are the most appropriate action based on where they are, as opposed to saying that one modality, model, or tool is the only way to do it all. I want to create a holistic theory of how the body works, both in terms of potential and in terms of healing the past, so we can be effective and efficient in our efforts.

THE TRIANGLE OF INJURY-RESPONSE-RELATIONSHIP

It may seem counterintuitive, but we need recovery *and* stress to survive. Let's take a simple example. When you exercise your body, you're putting it under stress, creating small microtrauma in your tissues. When you rest your body after the exercise, those microtears heal and then grow stronger in response and anticipation of more stress being added. In other words, you need stress and recovery for your muscles to develop. We'll tackle this in more depth in Chapter 6. Think of it as a Goldilocks zone, with one end being the right amount of stress and the other end the right amount of healing. If we move out of that Goldilocks zone, we suffer. Too much stress and we enter negative states; we climb down the nervous system ladder and stay between the second and third rungs. But too much time spent focusing on healing (as opposed to living our lives), and we stagnate. We don't grow. We need wounds to grow. Everything we experience has a function.

When stress falls outside the Goldilocks zone, we experience trauma. It's too much challenge, just like when you overexercise a muscle and injure yourself. If we keep experiencing this extensive amount of challenge, we live in this world of stimulus and response, and stimulus *in* response. This is especially hard when we're younger because our prefrontal cortex hasn't fully developed yet, so this stimulus-response process is happening without our awareness. It doesn't feel like it's happening *to* us; it feels like it *is* us, and we're in the thick of it. But when we grow up, our prefrontal cortex develops, which gives us the opportunity to be *with* our emotions rather than *in* them. We can be aware of those challenges that were outside the Goldilocks zone and that now need our help to heal.

But how do you heal from acute stress? The key is to improve your relationship to the injury. If you look at evolution, the species that have survived are not the strongest but the most flexible, the ones capable of adapting to change in their environment. Response is more important than brute strength. There has always been an inherent relationship between trauma and response, and response and healing. I like to call this the injury-response-relationship triangle. In one corner is the *injury*—the event that happened to you. In another corner is the *response* your system created to adapt to the injury and survive it. The third element is perhaps the most overlooked by many modalities: it's your *relationship* to the injury and to the response. The way you relate to your past and your adaptive responses is just as important to your healing as the traumatic event itself. *Improving your relationship to the injury is more powerful than only examining what happened to you.*

Recently, the world has become more trauma-conscious, which means there is more conversation around panic attacks, anxiety, and most disorders being trauma responses. I think that's fantastic, and there is real value in going back and exploring what happened to create these responses. But it can't stop there. Simply observing what created these responses lacks direction. You may understand the response, but what do you do with your understanding? For healing, we need to examine our relationship to those triggers and to the responses. That opens up space to say, *It's not the anxiety that's my problem, or the panic attacks, or the procrastination. It's my relationship with these things.* And the moment you say that, you have a starting point—a direction—for healing.

The point is not to minimize our emotional landscape. We want to make ourselves feel safer so we can live in a broader spectrum and have a richer emotional life. Many people suffer from *affect phobia*—a fear of emotions—where they think that if they're depressed or anxious, it's going to last forever. Learning how emotions move through us can be powerful, because we can let ourselves experience more joy and touch the evolutionary pulse of life. It gives us the freedom to take risks, because even if we feel depressed or anxious, we know we can come out of it. Our goal should be to be participants, not bystanders.

As human beings, we need a "why"—it's hardwired into our DNA. This is why purpose is so vital, because it motivates growth.

THE MYTH OF "THE WAY THINGS ARE"

When we're young, we're highly susceptible to social cues, authority, and social norms. As we grow, we begin to accept certain aspects of life and the world as immutable. We tell ourselves, *This is just the way things are.* We begin to decide what is or isn't possible for us.

As you begin your healing journey, I want you to interrogate those beliefs. I've asked so many clients "When did you decide this was the type of person you were?" or "Why did you think you couldn't do this?" and the answer is always rooted in their childhood and their development. But we're not children now, and many of those beliefs are not an accurate reflection of you or the world around you.

So, bring curiosity. Lead with it. Ask, "Why do I do this?" or "What could be the positive intention for this feeling?" Curiosity is the catalyst for growth. Without curiosity and a willingness to interrogate how things currently are, you can't really change. Curiosity is also the bedrock of scientific progress. When you think certain beliefs about yourself or have clear ideas of what you can and can't do, assume on some level you're wrong—even if you don't know why or how yet.

PART II

HOW TO GET OUT OF YOUR OWN WAY

CHAPTER 4

HOW YOUR NERVOUS SYSTEM ACTUALLY WORKS

"There is no such thing as a 'bad' response; there are only adaptive responses. The primary point is that our nervous system is trying to do the right thing—and we need to respect what it has done."

— STEPHEN PORGES, PH.D.

My whole life, I felt pain in my diaphragm that went unnamed and undiagnosed. It usually appeared in moments when I was trying to expand myself, like writing a chapter, giving a speech, expressing myself to the world, or asking for help. When the pain surfaced, I would shut down and lose my temper, without knowing why. It was just something that happened sometimes, and I carried a lot of shame about it. Over the years, I stopped being surprised by it, but I was acutely aware that it *didn't* happen to other people, which added to the shame. Clearly, I was somehow "bad."

A few years ago, I started doing serious therapy, and my therapist and I delved into this part of me. We discussed depression and abandonment, large terms whose definitions seemed to apply perfectly to me. My therapist also recommended I learn about Polyvagal Theory, so like the researcher and curious scientist I am, I explored the theory in depth.

That's when I discovered how the nervous system actually works. For years, we used to think that our autonomic nervous system was composed of two parts. One is the sympathetic system, which prepares the body for action and is often associated with our fight-or-flight survival responses. The other part is the parasympathetic system, which prepares the body for rest and its associated processes like digestion and healing. The theory of how these two parts operated was that when one part was on, the other part was off. Either your body was priming itself to respond to a threat, or it was headed toward relaxation. But when Dr. Stephen Porges introduced the Polyvagal Theory, he described how the vagus nerve, which is the body's live wire for the parasympathetic nervous system, actually branches out into two different parts— the ventral-vagal and dorsal-vagal branches.[1] The ventral-vagal branch is responsible for our social engagement and our sense of connection, community, and play—the comfort we receive from others. The dorsal-vagal branch governs our rest, digestion, healing, and growth, but it also modulates our "freeze" response—the impulse to shut down in the face of threat. When we are challenged, our nervous system automatically switches between these three different states or creates hybrid versions of them: ventral-vagal, sympathetic, and dorsal-vagal. Porges discovered we can even have all three parts of the nervous system on at once, in a sort of blended state.

Looking at diagrams of this system, I could see exactly where the pain in my diaphragm was coming from. It was right at the spot where the myelinated nerves of the vagal system stopped, and the unmyelinated nerves of the dorsal-vagal pathway began. The pain—and its associated emotions and thoughts—wasn't random, or unexplainable, or ridiculous: it appeared exactly where my nervous system switched into the dorsal-vagal response state. Polyvagal Theory gave me a map of my body that was so thorough I could pinpoint exactly what was going on in it. And the moment I did, the shame disappeared. Because I could name what was happening, because I now understood it, I realized my response wasn't "bad." My body was just doing what it was designed to do: protecting me.

Think about Joseph Campbell's *Hero's Journey*, when the hero is stuck in the belly of a whale. If you're going to be in that situation, it's much better to *know* you're in the belly of the whale than *not* know. It was the same here. Naming the problem didn't make the pain go away, but it helped me understand it. I realized I was the poster child for the "lone wolf" syndrome. My parents were great and did a lot of things right, but they assumed "he's smart, and he'll figure it out." I wasn't really shown the ropes on a lot of things, ironically, because of their confidence in me. And they were right; I did figure it out. But I also developed an inability to ask for help, so when I try to expand myself and reach out to the world, the pain appears. It's a protective response.

So much of what we call *disorders* is our nervous system switching between states in response to the level of challenge it perceives. Developing an awareness of those responses won't make them disappear, but it will help you learn the right amount of challenge you can take on without dysregulating your system.

THE LADDER OF TOLERANCE

Polyvagal Theory opened us up to the idea that our nervous system isn't just two systems but three, and that we don't switch between these states in on-and-off mode, but rather in a blended manner. Let's take a deeper look at what precisely this means, so you can have the same map of the body as I do.

Remember the ladder analogy from the last chapter? The bottom rung of the ladder is our dorsal-vagal system. This part of the parasympathetic system is located right below the diaphragm, and it creates immobilization (a.k.a. our "freeze" response). If you think of a turtle under attack, its response is to retract into its shell. That's exactly what happens to us in the dorsal-vagal state: we shut down and retreat into our shells; we hide. It's one of the oldest parts of our system.

The ladder rung above this is the sympathetic response, which is located primarily up and down your spine. So, at some point in our evolutionary history, instead of just hiding, we evolved to run or fight. We switched to a more active response than the dorsal-vagal system, creating what we call our "fight-or-flight" response.

The topmost rung of the ladder is our ventral-vagal nervous system, which is the newest part of our system and is parasympathetic. It's located above the diaphragm as the myelinated part of the vagus nerve. Myelin is a membrane that wraps around nerves, and as Stephen Porges describes, myelination around the ventral-vagus nerve "allows for quick and adaptive responses in social situations, promoting safety and connection."[2] It controls the variability of our heart rate (which is associated with the best health outcomes), breathing patterns, tone of voice, body posture, and facial expressions—in short, all the things that give mammals an edge. You won't see reptiles or spiders communicate nonverbally with facial expressions.

Over the years, human beings have evolved to cooperate with each other and function in groups using many of the tools given to us by the ventral-vagal system. Our prefrontal cortex, which is our most advanced machinery, is part of the ventral branch. When our ventral-vagal system and our prefrontal cortex are online, we function as our best selves in our most regulated state. We become calmer and less reactive. But when we experience load, we begin to move down the ladder, toward our sympathetic response and our dorsal-vagal state.

Early theories about our nervous system believed in a "window" of tolerance, which is the optimal zone of arousal for a person to function in everyday life. If you missed this window of tolerance, two things could happen:

- If you overshot it (you experienced too much load), you entered hyperarousal, where you were overwhelmed, out of control, and wanted to flee (for example, anxiety and panic attacks).

- If you missed it (you experienced too little load), you entered hypoarousal, where you were frozen, numb, and your body shut down (for example, depression).

I think Daniel Siegel is brilliant and the window of tolerance is phenomenal, but it was also introduced in 1999. It needs updating. We can see the flaws of the "window" theory when we look at a common experience people have when they're moving out of depression, which is that they move *into* anxiety. The window model assumes that they're moving from hypoarousal to hyperarousal and "missing" the window of tolerance. People going through this experience were "failing." But what we know now, thanks to Polyvagal Theory, is that shifting from a depressive, dorsal, red state to an anxious, sympathetic, yellow state is actually a shift *up*—and a natural, common one at that. Anxiety doesn't feel great, but it's a sign of the system starting to move. If we add Polyvagal Theory to the window of tolerance, it becomes clear we're not experiencing a window but a ladder, and we move up and down the ladder according to the load in our lives.

Green, Yellow, Red

This cumulative load—the pressures of our work and home lives, the challenges we embrace in our growth, the trauma we carry—is called our *allostatic load*. To get a sense of where your allostatic load is, and what changes it, think of these levels on the ladder like traffic lights: green, yellow, and red. We change states (a.k.a. "lights") depending on the amount of challenge and stress we're responding to. When we're in the ventral-vagal state, we're green. We feel playful, in the flow, even content or excited for a challenge. When we become stressed, we move down to our sympathetic nervous response and the traffic light changes to yellow. We feel agitated, upset, ready to pick a fight or leave the room. In America, we love the sympathetic response; most of us live in this state of constant yellow. When we encounter a threat we can't flee from or fight—like a life threat that we can't handle—we move down to the dorsal-vagal system and into the red. We freeze, we hide, we shut down.

THE RIGHT KIND OF STRESS

Our allostatic load is influenced by two kinds of stress: *distress* and *eustress*. Distress is unhealthy stress; it's when we experience a high threat level and we have no control. Eustress, however, is healthy stress. It's the load you feel when you take on a challenging task that isn't too difficult and that you believe will be rewarding. Many training models talk negatively about stress—but actually, what they're referring to is distress. Eustress is valuable and necessary, because it's how we build up tolerance, as we'll see in Chapter 6.

For now, think about load in terms of four criteria:

1. How much allostatic load is there (i.e., how much load has accumulated over time)?

2. How much control do you have?

3. How threatening does it seem?

4. How challenging is it?

Eustress is a moderate load with tons of control, low levels of threat, and a challenge that we perceive as rewarding. Imagine you're a really good Ping-Pong player and you have a friendly match against a worthy opponent. It will be fun, challenging, and with no downside—it doesn't really matter if you win or lose. Distress is the opposite: It's a high load with no control, high levels of threat, and an overwhelming level of challenge. It's playing a Ping-Pong match when you're really bad at the game, your opponent is your archnemesis and a national-level player, and the audience is your crush.

If you're living in the sympathetic (yellow) or dorsal (red) zones of your nervous system, you're not really making great decisions. You're just reacting based on emotions. There is a time and place for that, but you can't create your best life if you're always in the sympathetic or dorsal-vagal states, because you only focus on defending what you have, at best.

If you look at the mental health disorders in *DSM-5*, they are basically the hundred different ways in which your body can be in the dorsal-vagal or sympathetic nervous state, or a combination of the two. Depressive disorders are mainly dorsal-vagal (red) responses. Anxiety disorders are primarily sympathetic (yellow) responses. A bipolar disorder is a combination of a dorsal-vagal response and a sympathetic response, a blended state of red and yellow.

The state you're stuck in has a vast impact on your whole body. It can change your gene expression and your neurology, and it can cause your endocrine system and immune system to not function as well. It changes you.

Polyvagal Theory offers solutions. It recognizes that these shifts in state occur due to what has happened or is happening *to* you. These green, yellow, and red states are a response. The way to heal and optimize is to increase social engagement, reduce challenge, and work on being accepted for who you are. Understanding the traffic lights of your nervous system and the ladder of tolerance gives you a schema for how to do that: it builds awareness about your mechanisms of action for the ventral, sympathetic, and dorsal responses. Over time, you can predict if a situation is going to push you into the red or yellow zones, and then you can map your way *back* to the green zone through corrective actions you know will work for you.

A practical example of working your way from dorsal or sympathetic into ventral would be an entrepreneur who is just starting a business. This person can expect a lot of new challenges and stress in their life, so they know they are going into the dorsal-vagal or sympathetic states a lot to cope with that challenge. The way out of these red and yellow zones and back into the green is to delegate: to rely on a team to take on some of the stress. Many people try to biohack their way back into the ventral state with substances like nootropics, but the best hack ever is teamwork—which, let me tell you, is hard for me to say as a lone wolf. But it's true. The best way into the ventral zone is to share the load.

When I discovered the wonders of Polyvagal Theory, I reached out to Dr. Porges, the founder, and we developed a relationship. In 2017, we debuted Polyvagal Theory in coaching practice, and I'm pretty sure we are the first coaching company to do so. The response was incredible. There was an immediate sense of de-shaming; our clients went from believing something was "wrong" with them to understanding that this is how the body works and you can't blame it for doing its job. It's like shaming yourself for breathing in and out, or for having a digestive system. It's ridiculous. Once the shame was removed, they could lean more into their awareness. Before I created these processes based on the science of Polyvagal Theory, our clients felt like they were driving around in the dark trying to follow verbal directions. After Polyvagal Theory, it was suddenly daylight—they could see the road around them, and the directions made sense.

All of our clients felt this sense of calm that came from better understanding how they work emotionally. Better still, they could stay with their emotions, because their emotions were no longer the "bogeyman." Labels change our perception. "Panic attack," for example, is the worst name for the experience because the label is suggestive in and of itself, in such a way that it perpetuates the response. If you change that label to "I'm having a sympathetic response," the tone and suggestion are instantly different. You're anchored in the actual mechanism behind the experience and centered in your awareness.

We all have an intuitive connection to Polyvagal Theory, because we instinctively crave ways back to the ventral system. What our coaching does is give our clients the tools and knowledge to find their way to that state more effectively.

NEUROCEPTION

If we had to consciously analyze everything in our environment to determine if it was a threat, we wouldn't get very far as a species—it would simply take too much energy. This is why our nervous system has an unconscious threat detection machine that lives below the neck, known as neuroception. Think of neuroception as a radar system that consistently scans your environment to detect possible threats, but its processing occurs outside of your awareness.

This means that while it processes multiple sensory inputs—sights, sound, color—there is always a delay in you consciously recognizing the trigger. In other words, your body changes its state before you become aware. Say you're standing in the kitchen with your sister, and she makes a face you've come to recognize so well, a face that means she is disappointed in you. Instantly, your neuroception picks it up as a threat and your body changes states. But you haven't consciously noticed it; the expression was too brief or fleeting. You then leave the kitchen and walk into the living room, where you see your spouse. At this point, you start becoming aware of your triggered state, but you can't pinpoint what caused it. More often than not, you'll decide the trigger is your spouse and pick a fight with them.

This plays out in numerous scenarios. I had a client who felt unsafe in a session we were doing, so I paused, and we scanned the environment for what could be triggering her. It turned out that we had a red object in the office; she had seen it, been triggered, and then only realized she was triggered once the session had started, by which time she couldn't identify what had caused the destabilization. We got rid of the object and she was fine after that.

There are three types of neuroception, two of which are faulty neuroception (the third is, of course, when our neuroception is functioning well). The first type of faulty neuroception is when our body is in a safe environment but is unable to recognize this. Instead, it believes it's in a state of threat. Veterans with PTSD suffer from this, where their bodies believe they are still in the war zone, even though they're sleeping at home in their own bed. It makes it difficult to calm down or function properly. The second type of faulty neuroception is when you are in an unsafe environment, but your body perceives it as safe or ordinary. This is commonly seen in people in abusive relationships, where the abuse has been normalized. It can also be seen in the "deer in the headlights" phenomenon, where you freeze instead of fleeing in response to a direct threat to your life. "Freeze" is, of course, a danger response, but it's not the appropriate response for the situation. In essence, faulty neuroception is a mismatch between the environment and the danger response. Fixing that mismatch is key to bonding with people and establishing fulfilling relationships. As Dr. Porges says, "To switch effectively from defensive [dorsal or sympathetic] to social engagement strategies [ventral], the nervous system must do two things: (1) assess risk, and (2) if the environment looks safe, inhibit the primitive defensive reactions to fight, flee, or freeze."[3]

Our neuroception is also affected by the systems and environment we live in. In America, for example, differently colored bodies experience different levels of challenge and threat compared to white-bodied people. The foundation of American success was built on the back of slavery. Without slavery and the systems that support it, we would not have become an economic superpower. This is why racism is still alive and well today—because on some level, we believe we need it to prosper. Thus, when we say liberty and freedom, we often mean the pursuit of happiness for white men. The realities for people of color are very different from that ideal, because the economic, social justice, and law enforcement structures are biased against them. This means that people of color experience, on average, more day-to-day stress, danger, impoverishment, lack of equity, and lack of equality than white-bodied people do. White-bodied people have a certain level of privilege that allows them to be in a ventral state more consistently. Now, this doesn't mean that white people don't experience anything that pushes them into the dorsal or sympathetic states, because of course they do. But we have to move beyond binary thinking. There is a different level of stress placed on marginalized communities thanks to how the country is set up, and we must acknowledge it. For many people of color, there is a consistent living threat in how this country operates: socially, economically, and in terms of the law. Those signals of danger make it harder for them to exist in a regulated state.

This divide exists across genders as well. When I ask the women in my seminars how many of them have crossed a parking lot at night with the keys in their hands and on alert for danger, almost everyone raises their hand. When I ask the men, I've never seen a hand go up.

Much of why politics can be so polarizing today is because the same event is sending very different signals to different sections of the population. Donald Trump's tone, facial expressions, and body language were saying different things to people's neuroception depending on their background and how they were wired. To some, he seemed like a competent protector. To others, he came across as an abusive narcissist. Those who supported him followed his every move, but so did many of those who saw him as bad for the country—because they couldn't take their eyes off the threat.

A similar polarization is playing out with *Roe v. Wade*. It sent massive signals of danger to some and signals of safety to others. That's why it is so divisive and why arguments cannot meet in the middle: people are arguing in two different universes.

These kinds of sociocultural and environmental stressors impact a person's neuroception, and the consequences of this can be wide-ranging. Dr. Porges hypothesizes that faulty neuroception is possibly at the root of conditions such as autism, schizophrenia, anxiety disorders, depression, and reactive detachment disorder.[4]

BLENDED STATES

The first time I attended a gospel brunch was at Oprah's house. I remember being wooed by the soul and celebration of the culture, its spirituality. It also got me thinking: If you look at it through a polyvagal lens, gospel is a huge part of African American and Southern Baptist culture, and gospel singing stimulates and activates the vagus nerve. African American communities have experienced more stress than white-bodied cultures in America— as we saw in the last section—which means they're most often in the dorsal (red) or sympathetic (yellow) state. Gospel singing allows them to alleviate those states by stimulating the vagus nerve and introducing a ventral state (green). In other words, it makes them feel better. We could say gospel singing helps these communities create "blended states."

This is a powerful observation because it helps you transform your experience when you are in the yellow and red zones. In most stressed states, the green zone is offline. But you can bring it back online to create more combined states that make you feel better. This means that if you're in the yellow and you're anxious or nervous, you can introduce more green—through sharing with a friend, for example—and it becomes more playful. You shift the energy of that anxiety into excitement. Similarly, if you're in the red, you're usually depressed or have disassociated from events in your life. You can introduce more ventral/green by spooning your partner or meditating or doing an activity that puts you in flow. That way, you transform the same energy (being immobile and in one place) into a positive state where you feel safe.

Here's a great example: several of my clients are in the process of building businesses. Most of them come to me and say, "I can't do social media. I just can't. It's too scary." In seminars with these clients, I ask, "Who here has ever dissociated?" All hands always go up. I follow it up with "Who here has thought that the stuff they disassociated from was hard and painful?" All hands go up again. "Okay, great," I say. "Who here has felt like because you disassociated from that hard and painful stuff, it got you through it, but on some level it also made your life worse?" Without fail, all hands go up again. "Okay," I say. "So, since you're so good at disassociation, what if you just disassociate from how scary it is to do social media? Because at least then you're using disassociation to do something good for yourself." And it's an aha moment. Disassociation is a red zone: it's a subconscious detachment from the events in your life. It's not your choice. But what I propose to my clients is adding a little bit of green to that red to create "functional disassociation." It's disassociation with awareness so that it actually helps you. This choice is different from bypassing, in that you first acknowledge the parts of you that are scared and stuck in a survival response. If you choose to dissociate in the short-term, functional way to make your life better, you can train your system to know the new behavior is safe.

Here's how blended states work: we all have a piece of neuro-anatomy in our brains called the periaqueductal gray. When we're in a fight-or-flight situation (or perceive a fight-or-flight situation), the periaqueductal gray sends signals to the amygdala in our brain to trigger the appropriate response, putting us in the red or yellow zones. When we introduce green to those zones, either through awareness or actions that soothe us, our affective (i.e., emotional) triggers and somatic (i.e., physical) triggers "chill." The periaqueductal gray is deactivated and stops sending signals to the amygdala, which means our fight-and-flight machinery stops firing. Our prefrontal cortex gets activated, which is our most advanced anatomy and holds the majority of our opiate receptors, so we feel better. Simultaneously, our hippocampus is stimulated, which holds our historic memory, which means we no longer disassociate from the events but depersonalize from them: you are no longer *in* the experience, but *with* it. And that's powerful.

Ultimately, to introduce green into a red or yellow state, your prefrontal cortex must be activated. This means stimulating the myelinated, ventral side of the vagus nerve—as it is stimulated in gospel singing—because it regulates our heart rate, breathing, facial expressions, and tone of voice. How that activation happens is difficult to assert, because Polyvagal Theory is so new, but most often, you can create these blended states through awareness. Blended states can also occur outside of awareness, especially if there are cues of safety in your environment. Some people feel safe in the presence of another person, for example, and simply being near that person can inspire an unconscious ventral response.

Coregulation

When you're in the presence of someone who triggers an unconscious ventral response in you, that's known as coregulation. Polyvagal Theory defines coregulation as the sending and receiving of signals of safety. Let's look at this through the lens of co-dysregulation first, because that's often easier to grasp. We all have a person in our life whose tone of voice sets us off. They say something and boom—we're instantly triggered. In response, our body language and tone changes, because we're now in the yellow or red states. That's co-*dys*regulation. It's when we send signals of danger to each other. We don't know we're sending them, but our neuroception reacts to them. A lot of fights happen because we assume the other person is sending those signals *consciously*, when the reality is that our systems respond to each other underneath our awareness. Coregulation is the opposite of this. It's when someone's presence or tone of voice or smile puts us in a place of safety. It's when we're around people who naturally bring us into better regulated states (a.k.a. they introduce some green to our lives).

It's really hard to be in the ventral state without coregulation. As Dr. Porges says, "Coregulation is a biological imperative."[5] Ideally, we should always have one person in the room in the ventral state, so we can create spaces of psychological safety and coregulation. If everyone is in a sympathetic or dorsal state, it will just lead to consistent feedback loops of hidden stress.

The mental health community tells you, "If you can't self-regulate, we'll medicate you." The personal development community says, "If you can't self-regulate, then you must have a limiting belief or something must be wrong with you." What we know through polyvagal science is that we need to coregulate so we can be in a better state. Only then can we self-regulate. And that's not codependency, by the way—any more than saying we're codependent with air because we need to breathe. Codependency is when you cannot regulate yourself, and that person is your regulation strategy: whatever state they're in is the state you're in. Coregulation is when we send signals of safety to each other so we can feel better.

Let's say you're in a relationship and your partner just leaves one day. He doesn't tell you where he's going or why; he's just gone. A week later, he's back. Of course you will be worried and freaked out for that week. Now let's say your partner tells you he's going on a yoga retreat for a week, and he won't be in communication because he has to shut off his phone. You'll be much calmer about the situation because you've been told what's going on. The first version of that week sent signals of danger to you, while the second version sent signals of safety. That's coregulation. We're social creatures, and when we feel loved, accepted, and connected, we feel better. Naturally.

In my practice, I've often found that when people struggle with something, they struggle alone. They may have lots of help and friends, but for the specific issue they're struggling with, they haven't let anyone in. There's no coregulation.

If you look at all the great athletes or performers, each of them has someone. Tom Brady's relationship with his parents is paramount to his success, and he's very vocal about it. Michael Jordan's person was his dad: Jordan was so distraught when his father died that he quit basketball and joined baseball as a way to be closer to him. Dwayne Johnson has Dany Garcia, his ex-wife and manager. Oprah Winfrey has Stedman and Gayle.

Everyone has someone. I think that's really undervalued in this "self-achievement" world we live in, and it shouldn't be. There's no such thing as a "self-made" person.

A couple of years ago, I was in the emergency room visiting a friend who had just had heart surgery. The cardiac surgeon wasn't aware of Polyvagal Theory. When the nurse came in and tried to get the patient's daughter to leave, I thought to myself, *Fuck that. That's not going to happen.* I've been a patient advocate my whole life because my mom was always in the hospital. So, I went to the nurse and asked her if she wanted her patient to get better. She said of course she did. I told her about coregulation: that having someone the patient loved in the room regulates vagal tone, produces an eventual vagal state, and ultimately allows for additional growth and restoration.

"If you want your patient to get better," I told the nurse, "the daughter should probably stay."

I'll never forget the look she gave me: annoyed, exasperated, and irritated. "Fine," she said. "*She* can stay, but *you* definitely have to go."

I still laugh about that story. But it highlights two essential truths: coregulation is important, and Polyvagal Theory is hardly known among the wider medical community. When my father learned about Polyvagal Theory in 2019, he was educating his psychiatrist at Veterans Affairs about it. And we're still not close to mass acceptance of coregulation as a fundamental human strategy. This needs to change.

FOUR STATES OF SELF-REGULATION

What exactly is getting regulated (or dysregulated) when we shift states? There are four major areas of change that occur in our systems: emotions, somatics, mental or cognitive function, and social engagement. Let's examine how all four of these change in response to load.

Emotions

Emotions are a state of feeling. They are subjective and evaluative, which means that they embed an appraisal of what something means. When you feel a tightness in your chest, somatically, that's a physical feeling. When you ascribe the emotion of anxiety to it, you create an evaluation: anxiety is bad, and you begin looking for ways to make it better. That appraisal is entirely separate from the body and its sensations. For example, depression is different from a pit in your stomach, or stress is different from a clenched jaw. Bessel van der Kolk articulates this perfectly when he says, "The goal of emotion is to bring about physical movement to help us either get out of harm's way with negative emotion or to move in the direction of positive emotion."[6]

But what about those emotions we cannot articulate or understand? The medical name for it is *alexithymia*—that is, the inability to recognize your feelings and describe them in language, as well as an inability to distinguish between emotion and body symptoms. Alexithymia makes it easy for us to feel bad and difficult for us to feel good, because when we can't describe our emotions, our disconnection feeds our negative affect. In other words, we're not paying attention to what's happening inside of us—and as you know, the body needs our attention to get through a crisis.

The most common cause of alexithymia is the phobia of emotion. There are seven emotions human beings avoid: (1) versions of anger, assertion, or stress, (2) sadness, grief, or guilt, (3) attachment or closeness, (4) sexual feelings, (5) positive feelings toward one's self, (6) interest or excitement, and (7) joy. Avoidance presents itself in many ways:

- *I don't want to talk about my sexual feelings.*
- *I don't want to talk about how great I feel about myself.*
- *If I share my excitement, people cut me down.*
- *If I'm joyful, people won't celebrate me.*
- *If I'm close to someone, I'm not safe.*
- *I can't feel my grief.*
- *I can't assert myself and speak up.*

Our problems start when we inhibit these emotions rather than regulate them. Here's a quick breakdown of how your emotional state might map onto your nervous system and where you are on the ladder:

- Ventral-vagal (green) state: Passion, freedom, empowerment, appreciation, joy, positive expectation, optimism
- Sympathetic (yellow) state: Stress, anxiousness, blame, anger, revenge, hatred, rage, overwhelm, frustration
- Dorsal (red) state: Trapped, abandoned, depressed, powerless, disassociated

Somatics

Somatic is describing, relating to, or arising from the body rather than the mind. Broadly defined, it refers to bodily sensations in response to the environment. Think of it as kinesthesia, which is based on receptors in your muscles, tendons, and joints that enable you to know where you are in time and space. Without good somatic awareness, you're clumsy, have bad balance, or may walk into walls. Somatics keep you safe.

But how does this relate to trauma? According to Peter Levine, "We orient, dodge, duck, stiffen, brace, retract, fight, flee, freeze, collapse, etc. All of these coordinated responses are somatically based in the body. They are things that the body does to protect and defend itself. It's when these orienting defending responses are overwhelmed that we see trauma."[7] Common body responses to trauma include trembling, sweating, clenching, tingling, heart pounding, stomachache, chest pain, body heat, cold limbs, gut pain, and numbness.

Here's a quick breakdown of how your somatic state might map onto your nervous system and where you are on the ladder:

- Dorsal (red) state: You become hypoactive, which means you're passive, frozen, slow, withdrawn, and struggle to focus.

- Sympathetic (yellow) state: Your body becomes hyperactive, which can translate into restlessness, aggression, hyper-focused sweating, quick-fire responses, rapid movements, and reactiveness.

- Ventral-vagal (green) state: Your body relaxes, you feel calm and focused, and your body switches on mechanisms for health, growth, and restoration.

Mental or Cognitive Function

A good definition of *cognition* comes from the APA, which describes it as "all forms of knowing and awareness, such as perceiving, conceiving, remembering, reasoning, judging, imagining, and problem solving."[8] The most important thing to remember about this state of self-regulation is that it's essentially about thinking. Our thoughts come from our emotions and our body sensations, but this state is only looking at the thoughts (the mental symbols) themselves.

We think differently depending on which parts of our brain are online or offline. Executive function, which is our highest level of thinking, is controlled by our cortical brain. Creativity, decision-making, problem-solving, sequencing, task management, and organization are basically our prefrontal cortex in motion. Somatic awareness is controlled by our subcortical brain, such as our amygdala and our brain stem.

Here's a quick look at what our thoughts are doing, depending on the state of our nervous system:

- Ventral-vagal (green) state: Our prefrontal cortex is online, and we are able to see potential and possibility. We learn. The mind is calm and focused.

- Sympathetic (yellow) state: Our prefrontal cortex starts to go offline. We mobilize fight-or-flight mode, we become reactive, and we might start to enter a freeze state where we are stressed out but moving. The mind is racing and distracted.

- Dorsal (red) state: Our prefrontal cortex is fully offline. We zone out, we shut down. The freeze state enters into collapse, and we basically disappear. The mind is dissociated and checked out.

Social Engagement

A relationship is essentially an association between two or more people where there is an interpersonal link, and you have a degree of influence over each other's thoughts, feelings, and actions. The key word here is *interpersonal*—this category relates to you and other living things, even animals.

Here's a quick look at how our social state might map onto our nervous system:

- Ventral-vagal (green) state: We're pro-social and cooperative in relationships.

- Sympathetic (yellow) state: We move out of cooperation and toward defensiveness and aggression.

- Dorsal (red) state: We only experience people as dangerous.

This category is one of the most fascinating because we now know our brains depend on social relationships to help reduce allostatic load and make it easier to reach goals. In other words, evolution expects you to be in a group and trusts that this group will make things easier. Social baseline theory suggests that the hill is steeper and the distances further if you're fatigued, sleepy, less physically fit, stressed, or in a bad mood. But if you're close to social resources, the challenges become easier because your brain interprets social resources as oxygen and glucose and uses them as fuel. In other words, hills appear less steep when standing near a friend.

This is proven across studies. Socially isolated people consume more sugar because the brain treats social and metabolic resources as the same. Relationships enable load sharing and the distribution of risk, facilitated by familiarity, preference, joint attention, and trust.[9] This is why we seek groups that align with us. Short, safe, and transformational coregulation decreases allostatic load and helps regulate your nervous system.

WATCH YOUR TRAFFIC LIGHTS

Modalities that don't include working in the ventral (green) state won't work for healing. But if we can find a way to introduce the ventral state into what we're feeling to create a blended state, it opens up possibilities.

Dr. Porges has a saying: "Safety is the treatment."[10] Because without safety, you have nothing. Being in ventral (green) helps you feel safe, connected, and abundant; it's necessary for health, growth, restoration, and good relationships. When I tell my clients this, they often have a lightbulb moment, because they can see how they have lived their whole lives in the sympathetic and dorsal states (yellow and red) and how that impacts everything. What they were missing was green.

To effectively heal, we need to understand and observe our traffic lights. What state are we in, and why? Are we sliding or ascending? And how can we introduce a little bit of green to create a blended state that offers us more power?

I do the following exercise as a daily practice to help me better understand my different states. I'll walk you through the questions and my responses, so you have a schema for how to answer them yourself. Here are the first three questions:

1. Where do you feel green in your body?

    I usually feel green in my face and chest, and certain things in the environment cue that state: a good diet, being around nice people, a walk in the morning.

2. How do you feel when you are in green?

    When I'm in green, I feel abundant. I can solve almost any problem. I'm resourceful and a nice person. I'm friendly, super attractive, and more confident. I'm able to convince people to do things they don't think they can do so that they believe in themselves.

3. How does the world feel when you are in green?

    When I'm in green, the world is open to infinite possibilities. I see potential collaborations everywhere, and while I see problems, I also recognize that they have solutions that lead me to where I want to go. I see the world as progress and my purpose as adding value to it, not judging those I am sent here to heal. A world in ventral is a world filled with inherently good people, where my needs are met.

Next, we'll do the same evaluation for our sympathetic state:

1. Where do you feel yellow in your body?

    I feel yellow as a tension in my forehead, in the right side of my neck, and in my lower back.

2. How do you feel when you are in yellow?

    I have two different sides when I am in yellow: one part of me feels super angry and wants to blow shit up. I call him the "bomber," and I feel him more in my face than anywhere else. He doesn't care about my future, my past, my relationships; he just wants to blow everything up. It's a very sympathetic response that's like Fuck you, I don't need you.

3. How does the world feel when you are in yellow?

Another version of yellow for me is the belief that I'm on my own. No one is going to help or be there for me. I just have to keep going and pushing and hustling; otherwise, the world is never going to meet my needs. In yellow, the world is against me. It's full of ungrateful people who don't see what I do for them. I have to do everything on my own. I work harder than anyone else, and I won't ask for help because no one else can help me. I'm the only one who is capable, and I'm the only one who is right.

Now let's look at the dorsal state:

1. Where do you feel red in your body?

Red is in my solar plexus and below. It's also in my heart.

2. How do you feel when you are in red?

I feel sad, depressed, alone, and neglected.

3. How does the world feel when you are in red?

The world feels small, and it cannot meet my needs, even though I tried so hard. The world is full of people who don't see me and who will never show up for me, no matter what I do. In red, I am invisible.

When I'm in red, I'll probably check out, eat some sugar, and go to bed early. Then I'll wake up the next morning, tell myself I will do a lot today, but probably stay in bed and watch Netflix. I bet this sounds familiar. When the COVID-19 pandemic swept through the world, a lot of people were already living in a sympathetic state. Lockdown then moved many of us into the dorsal zone.

What's interesting about these states is they don't always feel like we think they will. A yellow state of "Fuck you, I'm just going to do it myself" can feel empowering. A red state of Netflix in bed all day doesn't always feel depressive; even though we're checked out and are in a dissociative mode, our brain can interpret it as "just chilling."

The more you do this exercise of nine questions, the better you'll understand yourself in these states. I think all of us have different answers, but the more you reflect on the questions, the more you'll tap into your own intuition about how your system works. You may have even recognized your patterns in some of my answers.

Interpreting Your System's Signals

While everyone's system has unique responses, there are common feelings and sensations that show up when we're in dorsal, sympathetic, ventral, and blended states. The descriptions below can help you map what you're feeling to the nervous system state your body may be experiencing:

- **Green:** Associated with calm, focus, social engagement, cooperation, and connection

- **Green/Yellow:** Characterized by excitement, determination, alertness, high energy, and readiness for action

- **Yellow:** Related to fight/flight, tension, nervousness, irritation, anxiety, and movement away from cooperative social engagement

- **Yellow/Red:** Represented by overwhelm, difficulty concentrating, and errors in work

- **Red:** Accompanied by fatigue, exhaustion, depression, entrapment, dissociation, immobilization, and fear of others

- **Red/Green:** A state of peaceful, dissociated immobility, as in restful sleep, meditation, and cuddling

Once we have a better gauge of where we're at (red, yellow, or green), we can potentially bring more awareness and start to blend states. Awareness is key. Even just knowing you have these states gives you tremendous power and agency—and that's a beginning.

CHAPTER 5

LET GO OF THE PAST, BE PRESENT, AND MOVE FORWARD

"You never change things by fighting the existing reality. To change something, build a new model that makes the existing model obsolete."

— R. BUCKMINSTER FULLER

I became friends with Dr. Frank Anderson by pure chance. I'd known about his work for years: he is a Harvard-trained psychiatrist, lead trainer at Internal Family Systems, and has worked with Bessel van der Kolk and Richard Schwartz for decades. In short, Dr. Frank Anderson is a trauma god. (He would disagree with this statement!) I consider him a genius (and he is), so I reached out to his assistant and tried to become his client. She told me his practice was full. A few months later, Frank got in touch with me completely out of the blue. He didn't even know I'd contacted his assistant until nine months after we started talking. We'd both been watching the Trauma Conference 2021 online; I'd followed him on Instagram, and it took one message from him for us to become fast friends. Through conversations that challenged both of us, we shaped a dynamic and powerful friendship. It's a rare occasion when a world-renowned psychiatrist and a college dropout are not only in the same room together but also have enough respect and curiosity to discuss issues from their differing perspectives. Frank has taught me a lot about healing; he's modeled what living from "self energy" looks like, and he compassionately challenges my thinking to be more rigorous and inclusive. When it comes to the things that Frank may have taken away from our conversations—you'll have to ask him.

What I love about Frank is that, in addition to his genius and super impressive knowledge base, he has humility, curiosity, and playfulness. A lot of people in the academic field have an ego that prevents them from being true scientists. It also makes them resistant to the concept of coaching, and I've had a lot of pain talking to academics about what I do because they are so closed to it. Frank isn't. It's been my experience that in the halls of academia and in the world of therapy, the word *coach* is a four-letter word. The dominant assumption in these spaces, it seems to me, is that only licensed professionals are qualified to work with trauma. After growing up with my dad—who had a doctorate in biology, was editor of a peer-reviewed journal, and taught me the scientific method—I find it oddly strange and unscientific that more people in academic communities aren't at least more curious about the outcomes my practice produces. Once, a leader in the world of trauma healing told me I had no business working with trauma until I went back to school to get my undergrad and master's degrees and underwent years of supervision. However, this person has never taken a seminar, retreat, or online program with us, or talked to any of our clients. The scientific method is based on the idea that anyone can form and test a hypothesis. I remember watching a MasterClass with Neil deGrasse Tyson, who explained that it's just as intellectually lazy to believe or disbelieve someone based on a claim they made without asking more questions.[1]

By contrast, Frank has modeled curiosity, openness, humility, and integrity in all of our conversations and debates. He once told me, "I like debating trauma knowledge and concepts with you. You've clearly put in the work to understand the field." I don't think there is a higher compliment he could have given me. Because if you're going to debate with Dr. Frank Anderson about trauma, the nervous system, and the brain, you'd better know what you're talking about. In one of our conversations, we were discussing the differences between therapy and coaching. I told Frank that a lot of therapy modalities deal with the past and the present. He thought about it for a while and said, "Mastin, you're right. I'm not aware of any therapy modalities that focus on the future."

Unlike therapy, coaching deals with the future. My job is to bring people into the future they want to create without allowing the past to interfere with their growth. But we need a practice that unites all three: past, present, and future.

Let's break down this concept so that it is easier to grasp. Trauma modalities you may have heard of, like Internal Family Systems, eye movement desensitization and reprocessing (EMDR), and Somatic Experiencing help you deal with the past. They sometimes give you more capacity in the present so that you can have a different future. But what these modalities do not take into account is the future itself, and how it may differ from the past and the present in terms of challenge and difficulty. A simple example is the entrepreneurial journey. Starting a business increases the difficulty in a person's life: the challenges and stressors they face in this future are not the same as the ones they face in their present or their past.

When you look at the trauma studies about the efficacies of modalities like EMDR and Somatic Experiencing, they don't take into consideration that this future can become more complex and dangerous. They assume the level of stress will remain constant. Yet this variable *does* change. And when it changes, it reactivates trauma pathways that many traumatologists will consider healed or released. Think of it like the game *Jumanji*. In video games, just as in a personal development journey, every level you ascend to gets harder and harder. The hurdles in the game, as in life, become more stressful, more complex, and more intense. You did therapy and trauma work for Jumanji Level One, but now you've evolved to Level Two and the challenges are entirely different. Of course, you're going to reactivate those pathways you thought you had "healed," because you're under intense pressure again, and when you take on more challenges, you react with a dorsal or sympathetic response (a.k.a. the red or yellow zones).

Increased complexity is a natural consequence of growth. Anyone who is single and has had their heart broken will face an increased level of complexity when they start seeing someone new (Jumanji Level Two). This complexity will keep increasing as they grow in the relationship: deciding to commit to each other is a new level of difficulty, as is buying a house or having a child or starting a joint business. We inherently make our lives more complex by facing more risk and uncertainty. It's natural. People think trauma modalities aren't working, but they don't realize they're increasing the load in their lives.

What is the difference between trauma modalities that build a person's capacity in the present with the hope that it will help them tackle the future, and accounting for the future in their healing process? It's like the difference between physical therapy and bodybuilding. In 2020, I couldn't walk for nine months. I felt a ton of pain in my feet, so much so that I could barely move them. My recovery wasn't just physical—we'll get into the mental, emotional, and spiritual aspects of it a bit later—but I needed physical therapy to help resolve that pain and be able to walk again. Once I reached a baseline of health, I progressed to weight lifting and strength exercises to build out the muscles in my feet. Now I walk 20,000 steps a day. Trauma modalities are like physical therapy. Coaching is like bodybuilding. You can't start conditioning or strength training without physical therapy. But physical therapy by itself is not enough: you need the conditioning to rebuild strength in your muscles to future-proof yourself against further injury.

This is what Frank and I realized in that pivotal conversation. True healing unites the past, present, and future. Each time you expand your vision for the future, your trauma responses—your past adaptations—will reactivate. To resolve these cycles in the present, you have to learn to work in a holistic way across all three time zones.

THE IMPORTANCE OF WORKING IN THE PAST

Your past is what has fundamentally happened to you, which is why it is such a big part of trauma work. Author and psychotherapist Resmaa Menakem says trauma decontextualizes mental illness.[2] Diagnoses like schizophrenia or borderline personality disorder or PTSD look at the symptoms, but they don't point to what happened to the person to create that experience. Bessel van der Kolk addresses this in his book *The Body Keeps Score*. He explains that if you put people with dissociative identity disorder—which used to be called multiple personality disorder—in a room in a hospital, they are bound to look crazy. But if you remove each person and place them back into their family of origin (i.e., the same environment with the same people) they will probably look like a genius dissociating from very hard circumstances. Out of context, it looks like a mental health disorder. In context, it's an appropriate response to the environment.

Trauma work allows us to have context, or "metadata," to describe why we do what we do now. The quest to understand why we act in a certain way is intuitive and valid. The simple answer to that quest is *because something happened to us*. Everything in life makes sense in the right context. If it doesn't make sense, you haven't found the right context.

Why do some people procrastinate on social media, for example? Because when they were younger, being visible or seen meant they would be abused, which means they have a subconscious link between visibility and abuse. Procrastination is their body's way of protecting them. The reason why this response is automatic is because decision-making takes a significant amount of energy, and the brain is trying to save them that cost. Trauma responses are shortcuts in our body's ability to make decisions that keep us safe.

Some trauma experts will say that it isn't necessary to regress and explore the past to fix a trauma response, but I argue that it's optimal. Let's return to the example of aerodynamics. In order for you to fly, you need lift, drag, and propulsion. The higher you climb in the atmosphere, the less fuel or propellant you need. If you think about how much energy it takes to break free of Earth's gravity versus how much it takes to get from the edge of Earth to Mars, you probably need less to get to Mars. That's because it takes an enormous amount of energy to lift free of Earth's pull. When you don't know what happened to you—when you don't work on your past to understand your context—there's friction and gravitational pull. There is energy you are using to hold on to that past or dissociate from it or not think about it. Working on your past may not be *necessary*, but it *is* optimal. You don't need it to fly, but you'll expend so much less energy once you do.

Caveat Emptor

A couple of years ago, my father introduced me to this Latin phrase. It translates loosely into: "Let the buyer beware." Regression work, when done safely, is incredibly healing. But if a person isn't safely regressed, they can be retraumatized. So many times, I've had people come up to me and say, "I've had a really bad experience with [insert a modality]." The first thing I ask them is, "Did you feel safe with the practitioner?" Their answer is always no. A lack of safety decreases the efficacy of any modality and increases the potential for traumatization. The problem, I tell them, is not with the modality, but with the quality of the relationship with the practitioner.

This is where caveat emptor is important. It is as Dr. Porges says: "Safety is the treatment." As a "buyer," pay attention to how safe you feel with a practitioner. Often that safety isn't there; it is not a given. Many times, consciously or unconsciously, we choose practitioners who will keep us exactly where we are because parts of us are not ready to move forward. Sometimes, we find ourselves attracted to danger because of a trauma bond. Sometimes it's just an honest mistake. Keeping ourselves open and aware of how much safety we feel will dramatically increase our chances of healing, because safety is 90 percent of it.

THE IMPORTANCE OF WORKING IN THE PRESENT

The day-to-day experience of living in your body is not comfortable. If you truly stopped to feel all the emotions and bodily sensations you experience minute by minute, you wouldn't like it. When I first started taking therapy seriously, I had a debate with my therapist about going slow. Anyone who knows me knows I move fast: I act, think, and speak fast—and they say this even though today I move about 90 percent slower than I used to function. I thought going slow was the dumbest idea I'd ever heard. I love my therapist; I think she's an absolute rock star. So why was she recommending something so obviously ridiculous to me?

"Mastin," she said. "The only reason you think it's ridiculous is because you don't know the value of going slow."

And she was right. I was like the *Millennium Falcon*, traveling through the universe at light speed. What I didn't know was that I had a magnet attached to my back that was pulling all this debris along—I never felt the weight of that trail because I was moving so quickly. The moment I slowed down, this debris slammed straight into that magnet and into me. It was *awful*. It was all those feelings and sensations I didn't want to feel: stress, worry, concern, abandonment, sadness, judgment, fear, physical pain in my body, disconnection. It was so uncomfortable for so long. I did not have a lot of metacognition, or self-awareness of how I do things. My interception, or my sense of my internal signals, was poor. And my radar for safe environments and safe people—my neuroception—was off.

By moving at light speed, I was trying to outrun my affect and my somatic awareness; I was trying to bypass them in action. It didn't work. The moment I slowed down, the emotions and the pain caught up with me.

I eventually realized the value of slowing down was that I could build better foundations—but it wasn't pleasant. It's so much better to not feel and simply escape into a vision of the future built with imagination. This is the dark side of being a visionary: we use visions of how the future could be to miss how we are right now. It can change the world, but it can also fuck you up before you have a chance to.

You have to work on yourself first.

People talk about the bliss of mindfulness and presence—no, thank you, I don't believe them for a second. Nobody wants to be present. What they want is to dissociate from what they're feeling in the present to either avoid it or find significance that can help them feel right. Stoicism, for example, is just justified avoidance. It's finding moral virtue in pushing your emotions far away. I think the present moment is really the hardest place for people to be. When you start trauma work, staying with those emotions and being in your body is miserable. So many of my clients tell me, "Mastin, I felt great before I met you. Now I feel like shit." Because they're finally feeling what their body and mind are telling them.

Wayne Dyer often came out onstage with an orange. He would hold up the orange and say, "If I squeeze this, what comes out?"

The audience would reply "juice."

"Great," he would say. "What kind of juice?"

The answer was obviously orange juice. The reason it's obvious? Because when you squeeze something, what comes out is what is inside.

When you do trauma work, it's like being pressed. The first emotions we encounter are the ones we don't want to feel. Believe me, I wish it were different. I wish we felt boundless joy and then eventually tackled the difficult terrain. But that isn't how it works—we reach the pain first, because the pain is what is inside. But staying in the present moment and sifting through those emotions *matters*. It matters because so many parts of you are trying to communicate with you right now. Your body, your somatics, your affect, your intuition. And it takes practice to build an improved relationship with those parts to hear what they're saying and stay in the present.

I've found that when you explore the past and work to release what you're holding, it makes it easier to stay in the present. The same is true when you have a compelling vision for the future that doesn't override your trauma. And over time, you'll have less of a fantasy that being present means being happier. Happiness is not the baseline. Many people believe that when they start trauma work they'll be more joyful, but that is a delusion. Think of what happens when you quit using drugs: you go through a detox first. The process of transformation is usually not joyful; that's what makes it so hard to be present.

Being present also means letting go of the past enough to start thinking about the future. That can be scary to a lot of people; they prefer talking about the trauma that has already happened to moving into the future and potentially creating new trauma. The devil you know is better than the devil you don't. This is also where the fear of success comes from. If you break it down, people fear re-creating a painful circumstance in their past, or being abandoned, or facing disapproval. Perhaps they feel they will be overwhelmed with more success, or that success will bring changes their family caregivers won't approve of and will lead to isolation from the tribe. It's always more about the relational pain than it is about the success itself.

Befriending the Present, Moving into the Past

Befriending the present and staying with our emotions makes it easier to examine the past. It becomes simpler to work through our trauma. Trauma triggers are uncomfortable, and most of us want to avoid pain. When we encounter pain, our first instinct is to minimize it. But the more we're able to manage the pain and reside with those emotions, the more we can connect to them. I'm talking about both psychological connection and new neurological wiring. These connections offer us a sense of wholeness. Being present leads to healing because by bringing attention to what causes us pain, the solution often presents itself.

Being present helps us tap into the body, which knows where we need to go to heal. Osteopathic philosophy, for example, believes the position of trauma is often the position of healing. When we have a physical injury, our fascia will prevent us from going back into the position that caused the injury because it believes it is not safe. And so a lot of osteopathic and myofascial work is helping the body not only release but also return to positions of trauma safely, so it can learn that the position is not always dangerous.

When we learn to befriend our pain—whether it's physical, somatic, affective, or emotional—we can pay more attention to it. And the moment we pay attention and listen to what it is telling us, it reveals something from our past that is key to healing. For a long while, my foot pain was undiagnosable by the best doctors in the world. It was driving me crazy. I was used to looking up a problem and figuring out the solution, but there was no diagnosis for this, no matter how hard I looked. In 2020, my left ankle was on fire. I couldn't walk, which is primarily how I give seminars; I couldn't even stand well enough to play virtual reality. And I reached a point where I said to myself, *I'm just going to sit with this.* No pain medication was working anyway. So, I drew a bath and sat with my ankle in the bathtub, just being with it. And it started showing me memories. I don't know how long those memories played for, but it felt like a two- to three-hour journey. It was a life review of all the times I'd been neglected, as if those memories had been stored in my ankle. It was awful—I was crying, snot running out of my nose, shaking uncontrollably, and holding myself—but I sat with it because I'd done enough trauma work to bear it. By the end, I said to my ankle, "You know what? If I were you, I wouldn't want to go on either." Forty-five days later, the pain cleared, and I haven't had pain since.

My ankle was asking me to pay attention to it. It drove me to my knees—absolutely stopped everything I was doing—to get that attention, because all I was doing was injecting pain medication into it and taking anti-inflammatories. The work I had to do was just be with it—not analyze it or plan how to fix it, but listen and watch what came up. Once I did, my body showed me what I needed to see.

The most valuable asset is attention. It's what our children and our partners want, and it's what our bodies want. I coach a lot of heteronormative couples, where the guy is typically more masculine, and in those dynamics, the couple often describes to me how the man doesn't have an emotional or physical presence in his relationship. I joke with them that there are two types of "presents": being-there presence and gifts presents. But the second kind of present won't work without the first. It's a joke, but you'll be surprised by the number of male clients I have who are startled by the money they could have saved by just being present. I was no different: I spent about three to four hours sitting with my ankle, compared to years of ignoring it and plying it with "solutions."

Think of the physical pain and emotional pain in your body as relationships you have with parts of yourself. Listen to them. Pay attention.

THE IMPORTANCE OF WORKING IN THE FUTURE

When I think of the future, I always come back to a seminal line from the Bible: "Without a vision, the people perish." A compelling future is a fundamental motivator. If we don't think the future is going to be better, there's not much to live for. When we work in the future time zone, we're essentially thinking about our life purpose. We often explore the following questions when I engage in future work with my clients. Feel free to jot down your own answers as you read:

- *What is your purpose?*
- *How do you want to feel?*
- *What part of your life do you want to start making changes in (business, relationships, etc.)?* Most people start with business, because if they change their business, they change their money, and that affects a lot in their life.
- *What's your goal?* It's not uncommon for people to say they want to quit their job or outline how much money per year they want to make as a coach or a consultant.
- *What are the specifics of that vision?* Here, we deep dive into the details: how much money do they want to make and by when, what exactly will they be selling, etc.
- *What motivates you?* These are the specifics of why they have chosen that vision and what will keep them moving toward their goal. People usually say they want to prove their supporters right or prove their naysayers wrong. Some talk about setting

an example for their children. Others lean in to a higher mission or a calling that inspires them to do something beyond themselves. Still others see themselves as functioning as a transitional character, a person who stops passing down generational trauma to their lineage (more on that in Chapter 11).

Once you have your motivators, it's time to plan your vision. This includes the behaviors, habits, and routines you need to achieve your goals.

- *While you work on creating this vision, what parts of your past do you think are dangerous and can hold you back?* You must create a plan to work with them as you move forward so that they're not stopping you for as long.

The last point is vital, because it helps you handle parts of yourself that will be triggered when you move into the future and face increased complexity; they are the parts of you that will wreak havoc. Being aware of them helps you build capacity to manage increased challenge. When I talk about these aspects of the past, I often receive the criticism "You're just being negative." But I'm not; I'm being aware. And that awareness can make all the difference.

When I step into expansion mode, I have a little guy in me who believes my plans are not going to work out or no one is going to show up. Each time this guy starts to speak up, I know I am officially expanding, and an old fear is rearing its head. This awareness creates a very different context from just believing my plans won't work. If I believed this little guy, then there is a chance I would take what he says and make it a self-fulfilling prophecy. I don't believe in the term *self-sabotage*; I don't think anyone wakes up and thinks, *I can't wait to sabotage myself.* But I do believe that old parts of you speak up just before a change or big success, because they believe the next level might be dangerous. This is why we see so many people on the verge of success who ruin it.

I don't know what was going through Will Smith's head during the 2022 Oscars, but I can hypothesize. He had to have been dreaming about that moment for most of his life; it is every actor's dream to win the Best Actor Oscar. But right before he was about to win it, he got up, went onstage, and slapped Chris Rock. Bear in mind that this is Will Smith, one of the most upstanding actors around. I don't know of anyone before that incident who would have said Will Smith is a jerk. To me, that just screams that some part of him does not feel worthy of that success. That's what we mean by *self-sabotage*—and I don't know of anyone who doesn't do it.

Be aware of those parts of you that speak up and push you to stop or stay small. They need you to be their friend through that change, or they will look for ways to pull the emergency brake on you.

Handling a More Complex Future

The point of working in all three time zones is to help create more capacity to handle the future as it arises, with all its elevated complexity. When you work in the future, the protective parts of you are going to speak up. Your goal should be to reduce the frequency, intensity, and duration of those conversations. If you map this onto what we discussed in the last chapter, this means the frequency, intensity, and duration of your yellow and red zones will reduce, and you will have more space for green. As you move forward, you increase your capacity for uncertainty, which elevates the ventral, optimistic, and joyful parts of you and reduces the barriers that may be holding you back. The best way to do this is to move forward with purpose.

The definition of purpose I love the most comes from a paper by McKnight and Kashdan. It reads: "Purpose is a central, self-organizing life aim that organizes and stimulates goals, manages behavior, and provides a sense of meaning. Purpose directs life goals and daily decisions by guiding the use of finite personal resources."[3] Purpose helps us answer questions about who we are, where we're going, and what we're doing. To me, purpose is our emotional immune system.

We live in a violent universe; there is no escaping that fact. But purpose can make a lot of unbearable things bearable. I've seen this in my practice. I've had clients who have endured awful experiences in their lives, and when they finally find purpose and meaning, it can redefine that worst moment into a useful and powerful incident that functions as a transition point. Purpose has the capacity to create transformative change because you find a different meaning.

To be clear, one way to hurt yourself more is to assume your trauma happened for a reason. Trauma is not a lesson, or a gift. Trauma is not something you decided to have before you got here on this earth. Trauma *happens*. Finding purpose *from* trauma is different from finding the purpose *of* the trauma. The prepositions are important: One denotes an external locus of control, while the other allows you to take responsibility for the future you build. Your choice lies in what you do with the experiences you've been through; in that choice is where you can find your purpose and your power.

One client I worked with had been subjected to satanic ritual abuse growing up. For the first 10 years of her life, she'd been repeatedly and brutally hurt by a circle of men. She'd lived much of her adult life with a poverty mindset. Her orientation came from not wanting to be seen: if she became successful, she might be more visible; if she became visible, she would get hurt. The imprint they'd left on her nervous system was still there. When she realized the impact of what they had done to her was still affecting her into her 60s, she made the choice to start her own business. Choosing to continue participating in the trauma pattern of poverty meant that the men who hurt her still had influence over her. As she became more regulated, stronger, and resilient, she chose to opt out of this programming by finding new purpose in it.

In *Learned Optimism*, Martin Seligman asks, is the trauma "personal, permanent and pervasive"?[4] These are the three questions we ask ourselves for each experience. By personal, we mean, "Is it about me, or is it about the world at large?" By pervasive, we're asking, "Did this just happen to me, or does it happen to everyone everywhere?" And by permanent, we're trying to judge if its effects are forever or short term. Purpose in life helps us understand that we're not stuck the way we are; the current conditions are impermanent. The problem isn't pervasive; it was just a specific moment. And you didn't deserve this trauma, but it is your responsibility to heal it.

I've seen clients who believed they were abused because they deserved it. Once they do the trauma work and find their purpose, they're able to see the difference between their responsibility and someone else's. They recognize that while it wasn't their fault they were abused, it is in their power to heal from it. It reframes the experience from something awful to something that's now also powerful and transformative.

Purpose creates meaning and context to make things not only survivable but also useful to our evolution. A large part of being an optimist is realizing that your problems aren't just about you, nor are they the entire universe, and they won't last forever.

A client who was a schoolteacher once asked me for advice about one of her students. As she described the school environment they were in, I could tell there wasn't much that the teacher could do to help her student. The school system was bigger than this individual teacher. I noticed she became dysregulated—upset and agitated—as she described how she couldn't help this student, and how just recently she'd lost another student to gun violence. It's a tragedy anytime we lose someone, and especially a child, to gun violence. However, as her coach, I wasn't paying attention to the morals she was struggling with; I was trying to serve the individual in front of me. I noticed she had personalized the event: *she* had "lost" the person, and some part of her seemed to think it was because of her own efforts that the child had died. Of course, there was nothing she could have done. After some questioning, I learned she had lost many family members in her history, including her primary caregivers when she was young. She had never considered that the loss she had experienced when she was younger was alive in her today as an adult teacher.

Her fear of loss was driving her to try to save children in a school system and a socioeconomic environment far stronger than her. No person alone can change a zip code, and she couldn't save 1,300 students alone. In the clinical space, we call the effect she was experiencing "countertransference." Transference happens when a client is triggered by something the practitioner says; countertransference occurs when the practitioner is triggered by what their client brings forth. The practitioner's own history presents itself, just as her own history was coming up in response to her students. I guessed the grief she hadn't processed from her childhood was being reenacted daily at this school. As a schoolteacher, she didn't make much, yet she invested vast sums in her education and coaching with us. This detail told me she had ambition beyond her current environment. But for some part of her, moving forward to start her own business would mean giving up on 1,300 kids. Past grief, playing out in the present, was preventing her from creating the future she wanted.

It was a beautiful awakening for her to get in touch with the grief and loss of her past. She saw how her grief showed up in her noble intentions to save her students. And in a stunning moment of sobriety, she acknowledged she couldn't change the school system, the local economy, the laws of the county, or the laws of the country. She realized she could love and want to care for all her students—for the whole world—but if she wasn't whole, she wouldn't do the good she wanted to do in the world. Seeing the continuity of past, present, and future gave her the power to make a different choice. She started her business, with more self-compassion and less shame around letting go of the dysregulating environment from which she'd grown.

BE KIND

Healing happens by improving your relationship to your past, present, and future. It is the work in all three time zones that helps us deal with the increased challenge of our future and lean in to our growth. Nervous system work, purpose work, and trauma work are lifestyle choices. We don't go to the gym once and expect to be a perfect weight; we know that's a lifestyle change. It's the same with trauma work. It's about training and regularly practicing these philosophies. Moreover, when you graduate to the next level—whatever that is for you—it's almost like you start from the beginning again, with more skill and capacity to build. I don't say that to be pessimistic, but to really show you how intrinsic and embedded this change needs to be. Say you're a runner and you just hit a personal best time. Or you lift weights and you just set your new personal record. Do you stop? No. Your instinct is to move to the next milestone, and then the next, and then the next.

We are built with this constant, never-ending human desire for growth. It's a valid desire. But it also places more pressure on your system, because you're moving into a future that's uncertain and with increased complexity. You can tackle this if you see this work as a lifestyle shift. It's not a pill you take to make the pain go away; it has to be an emotional fitness regimen you'll commit yourself to from now on.

Be proud of the work you have done so far, because it *has* worked. You're just moving from one stage of *Jumanji* to the next, and that means increased challenge. Have more compassion for the hard work you've put in so far, and be kinder to yourself. Life is an epic journey; you are simply learning how to navigate it.

CHAPTER 6

REDUCE UNCONSCIOUS STRESS—
AND BE MORE PRODUCTIVE

"The best moments usually occur when a person's body
or mind is stretched to its limits in a voluntary effort
to accomplish something difficult and worthwhile."

— MIHALY CSIKSZENTMIHALYI

When I was young, penniless, and couch surfing, Tony Robbins changed my life by inviting me to his seminar "Date with Destiny." I'll be honest: I was turned off by the sales pitch. But I met with him and his wife later in the week, and they repeated the invitation with so much passion I knew it wasn't just about sales for them. Well, obviously it wasn't, because I was penniless and couldn't pay. It showed me just how much they cared about what they were saying, so I went to the seminar—and it changed my life.

I've talked about the impact of Tony Robbins and that "Date with Destiny" in my first book, *Daily Love: Growing into Grace.* But what I didn't mention is that when I started out speaking and coaching, people often compared me to Tony. I didn't quite know what I was doing then. Functional Life Coaching™ hadn't been born yet, and the journey to get there would be long and circuitous. But I did know one thing: I didn't want to be the next Tony Robbins. I wanted to be the first me.

Fast-forward 10 years later. We were doing an event with Sage Event Management, and their co-founder Bari Baumgardner; my business partner, Jenna; and I were trying to figure out what exactly we were offering to our audience. Bari has this superpower to read the room and know what will give the most value to participants. And she was really pushing us to niche down and clarify our products and offers. But I couldn't. I couldn't pick between a trauma lane and a business lane and a self-development lane. I didn't know how to define what we did. I remember admitting to both Bari and Jenna how difficult I found this . . . and how frustrating it was for me. Bari looked at me with so much compassion and said, "Mastin, it's difficult because you two are doing something that's never been done before."

In that moment, something clicked for me. I'd been so focused on being myself—on offering what was uniquely me—that I had forgotten it was *unique*. I wasn't wandering down some well-walked path with rest stops and signs and guidebooks written by people who had been there before. I was on Mars, and there was a tent in the corner and one bottle of water. *Of course* it was hard. How could it not be?

Bari helped us realize that the difficulties we faced weren't because we were doing something wrong but because it was new. The moment I realized this, my nervous system relaxed, and I stopped facing so much resistance, because that's when we realized our approach was functional: we simply couldn't view each part in a silo.

You know from the last chapter that the future always holds a higher level of challenge. You may not be on Mars with a tent and one bottle of water—it may not be *that* difficult—but it certainly won't be territory you've traveled before. You can handle this new future by increasing capacity. Here's the big opportunity: You can grow your capacity and achieve or even exceed your dreams—if you know how to work with your nervous system. The key? Creating the right level of challenge. Too much challenge is dysregulating to the system. With greater self-awareness, you can set better expectations for yourself and take on the right level of challenge to build your capacity.

THE POST-TRAUMATIC GROWTH MODEL

Have you ever hit the gym hard? If you have, you'll know that 24 to 48 hours later, your body hurts. This pain is natural and, in fact, beneficial: it's how you build muscle. Let's call this a type 1 injury.

Now imagine you've overdone it at the gym and have torn your muscle. We're not talking microtears (type 1 injury) but a complete tear of the muscle and fascia. That's a type 2 injury and can lead to lasting damage. No one wants a type 2 injury.

There is a third category of injury, where your muscles feel sore immediately after exercising. These type 3 injuries are not disabling, but they signal to you that you should pause and massage out the problem. Pay enough attention, and a type 3 injury will not become type 2.

Why are we talking about exercise and muscle injuries? Because building your capacity for trauma and growth looks a lot like bodybuilding. To understand how this analogy works, let's look at how muscles are actually strengthened. There are four components to bodybuilding: training, microtrauma, nutrition, and recovery.

Training is the lifestyle of challenging your body the right amount. You can't fill out your biceps if you never go to the gym or look at a dumbbell.

Microtrauma is how your muscles are built. A good level of exercise leads to type 1 or type 3 injuries, which are little tears along your muscles. When those tears heal, they increase your capacity to handle load. The biological term for this is the *repeated bout effect*. Have you ever heard of eccentric strength training? It's where you slow down a movement to reap more benefits from lengthening the muscles under load. The microtrauma created from a single bout of eccentric strength training can help your muscles adapt and protect themselves from subsequent eccentric bouts (a.k.a. the repeated bout effect). In simple terms, the more you practice within safe limits, the stronger you become. The stronger you become, the harder it is to hurt you. Remember that microtrauma is linked to type 1 or type 3 injuries. Type 2 injuries can cause damage; they are not strengthening but debilitating.

Nutrition is key to fueling the process of muscle repair—so the right balance of carbohydrates, fats, and proteins.

And lastly, recovery is fundamental to building muscle. People think that lifting weights is what makes you stronger, but in fact the real magic happens afterward. Weight lifting is the catabolic process, where you break down the muscle through microtrauma, but you won't strengthen your body unless this is accompanied by the anabolic process, which is when your muscles heal and are rebuilt. Rest and recovery are not indulgences; they are necessities. If all you do is exercise without giving yourself a chance to recuperate, you don't get stronger—you just get injured.

Developing Your Nervous System

Here's where it gets interesting: the same process of training, microtrauma, nutrition, and recovery applies to your nervous system. There's a phenomenon called *pendulation*, which is the expansion and contraction of your body sensations and emotions. Through pendulation, you can regulate the ebb and flow of your emotions and somatic experience between polarities, such as safety and danger, stress and calm, depression and happiness. Think of pendulation as having control over or being able to regulate your experience, which facilitates the deep integration of these polarities. Integration is impossible, however, if you spend too much time in distress or in safety. Extremes don't help us. You need the right level of exposure—exactly like bodybuilding.

Let's look at the different types of injury again, but this time from the lens of the nervous system and the ladder of tolerance. Type 1 injuries are what I call *delayed onset* affective, somatic, mental, and relational ruptures that occur with safety. Sometimes, we're triggered by an event but don't realize it until much later through neuroception. When we do realize the trigger, we are in a position of safety and have the chance to repair it. A type 2 rupture is a disabling affective, somatic, mental, and relational rupture that can't be repaired and creates less nervous system capacity. These are complex traumas or shock traumas that occur without safety. Type 3 ruptures are affective, somatic, mental, and relational ruptures that you're aware of in the moment. These can be repaired and build more nervous system capacity.

In the same way different people will experience a heavy weight as heavier or lighter depending on their strength, everyone experiences traumas differently, depending on their relationship to them. What makes a rupture type 1, 2, or 3 is not the event itself, but the impact the trauma had on the individual. A dramatic event like a divorce might be a type 2 injury for one person, while another person can't wait to get away from their ex-spouse and experiences the divorce as type 3. We're complicated beings with layered experiences, and no experience lands the same with us all.

In the past, you've probably experienced type 2 ruptures—a.k.a. trauma—which is why it's easy for your nervous system to think type 1 and type 3 ruptures are the same as type 2. But they're not. Just like muscle building, we need type 1 and type 3 ruptures to build emotional fitness, while hopefully reducing and eliminating type 2 injuries. If we don't delineate the nuance of these different injuries, we miss out on the opportunity to grow. Of course, true growth occurs with balance. This is where titration comes in.

Titration is a term Peter Levine, the developer of Somatic Experiencing, borrowed from chemistry, and it is an approach where a person can gradually access the energies and body sensations that have been stuck.[1] We don't do it all at once, but instead a little bit at a time. You want to experience tough emotions with safety that doesn't drop you down the ladder for too long. You don't go too far too fast.

Essential to this whole process are proper nutrition and recovery. So even while you're exposing yourself to type 1 or type 3 ruptures, you need adequate "nutrition"—or resources—to help counteract that exposure (we'll explore these in a minute).

Recovery (a.k.a. shifting back into ventral/green mode) is fundamental to increasing capacity so you can do this again. Because if you never recover, you're always challenging yourself, which can eventually turn type 1 and 3 ruptures into type 2.

Affective, Somatic, Mental, and Relational Nutrition

It's easy to see how nutrition is vital in the context of bodybuilding; without the right diet, we don't have the necessary ingredients to grow our muscles. But what does this look like in the context of our nervous system? Think of "nutrition" here as internal resources, strengths, and positive memories that soothe the nervous system and strengthen the resource that's being activated. How does it work? Building on the work of EMDR founder Francine Shapiro, Dr. Scott Giacomucci explains, "Because the nervous system can't always differentiate between a dream, a memory, a real-time experience, or an imagined experience, we can use positive resources to regulate our emotions and reduce the impact of trauma on our life today."[2] In other words, the brain cannot tell the difference between imagination and reality, both in the context of trauma *and* healing, which allows us to rewire them through positive thinking. Why is this important? Because so many people wander into trauma work and healing without realizing they aren't prepared to face difficult emotions, and they wonder why they feel so poorly. The solution, they imagine, is to get rid of triggers altogether. But, as we just discussed, some types of ruptures are good for us. The solution to those difficult feelings we experience when we drop down, from ventral (green) into sympathetic (yellow) and dorsal (red), is to develop self-regulation skills that help us deal with those emotions. These skills or techniques are what we call "resources" or "nutrients." They are how we cope and stay in a zone of safety.

Here are the five most common resources you can call upon when you're in the middle of a tough emotion and doing the work:

1. **A safe place** (real or imagined) where you are by yourself. For me, it's a beach in Maui, but it could be a place in the clouds with Care Bears—whatever is a safe space for you.

2. **Nurturing or protective figures** (real or imagined). These could be role models, archetypal pop-culture figures, superheroes, angels, Buddha, or Jesus.

3. **Animal resources** (real or imagined).
   This could be a pet you love, a phoenix
   rising from the ashes, or a unicorn.

So, imagine yourself in a safe place, with a safe person and safe animal—automatically, this will change your response to the difficult emotion. Now:

4. **Imagine a container.** Take your reactions
   and emotions, and imagine yourself placing
   them in the box. This isn't about overriding
   or repressing an emotion, but taking back
   control over a feeling that was controlling
   you. Think of it as drawing a boundary.

5. **Do some form of bilateral stimulation.** This is
   any activity that uses both sides of your body in
   motion. This could be back and forth tapping,
   eye movements back and forth, or listening to
   bilateral sounds. You can dance, sway back and
   forth, alternate squeezing each hand, toss a ball
   back and forth, draw with both hands, or breathe
   through one nostril and then the other. Walking
   is bilateral stimulation, as are sports and weight
   training. These activities help calm the nervous
   system and keep you grounded, neutral, and calm.

Why bilateral stimulation? The answer to that question could be an entire book. The bottom line is that bilateral stimulation promotes communication between the left and right hemispheres of the brain. By definition, when your left and right sides are talking more, that's integration. If I notice someone gets a little stiff when talking about the past, I have them touch each finger to their thumbs on both hands. If they tell a story while looking fixedly up and to the right, I have them retell it looking down and left.

Without getting too into the science, bilateral stimulation tends to activate the motor cortex of the brain. The motor cortex is part limbic, part prefrontal cortex; I think of it as the gateway between the prefrontal cortex and the limbic system. Using the whole body in motion helps regulate limbic responses—after all, you can't be frozen and moving at the same time. We know that sensorimotor rhythm brain waves, which are low-beta brain waves between 12 and 15 hertz, are associated with calm alertness, brain plasticity, and reduced hyperarousal, anxiety, inhibited impulsivity, hyperactivity, and maladaptive behaviors that result from trauma.[3] In short, bilateral stimulation helps you tap into your experience in a way that's fun, playful, and resourced.

Can you see how these resources help you work through tough emotions? There are also an additional five layers of resources you can tap into:

1. Environmental resources (safe places and environments)

2. Social or relational resources (safe people and relationships)

3. Emotional resources (creating safe feelings in your body)

4. Somatic or body resources (safe body positions, and releasing tension, like unclenching your jaw or softening your gaze)

5. Cognitive resources (safe thinking and safe self-talk)

The last resource I want to leave you with is the butterfly hug. This is where you wrap your hands around your body and tap your shoulders, which is a great technique for people who are not in their bodies. The purpose of all these techniques is to bring a sense of safety, comfort, and calm to your present experience. Do what works for you.

The Myth of Perfect Regulation— and the Cycle of Emotional Fitness

Everyone wants to be in a ventral state. It's the state in which we feel the happiest—we're in flow, living in the green zone, and we're joyful. What more can we ask for, right? But one of the most beautiful gifts of Polyvagal Theory is that it's built to help us grow capacity. This means that when something in our life gets harder, we drop down from ventral (green) into the sympathetic state (yellow). But that act of dropping down gives us the opportunity to build back up to ventral—with increased capacity. The problem arises when people try to avoid this drop—when they want to be in ventral all the time. Perfect regulation is not only a myth, but also it's not good for you over the long term. Jenna likes to joke that if someone's goal is to be perfectly regulated at all times it actually ends up being more like they are "violently regulated," instead of creating a more flexible nervous system.

There is a cycle of emotional fitness: we regulate, we dysregulate, and then we regulate again, just like building muscles. Then, as we grow stronger, we take on more load and begin the cycle again. You have to make sure you're prioritizing your safety and limiting the window of exposure to what you can handle. But if you focus on your welfare, draw on the appropriate resources/nutrients, and ensure plenty of recovery time, this cycle is how you create a better life.

Remember that the post-traumatic growth model is not about healing from acute trauma (type 2 ruptures). If you're looking to do foundational work, then you must turn to other resources. This structure is for post-traumatic growth. In other words, once you've done your base work, we want to help you expand and grow beyond your current limits.

Finding the Right Amount of Stress

The cycle of emotional fitness depends on us choosing the right load for our capabilities in order to build capacity. In Chapter 4, we talked about distress and eustress, where distress was negative challenge and eustress was positive challenge that exists within our zone of capability. The Yerkes-Dodson curve defines the zone of optimal performance between eustress and distress—in other words, an optimal stress level that helps develop strength. This is the optimal level of challenge we are chasing. It's important to note that it varies between individuals, so what works for one person won't work for another. Most of us try to tackle too much too soon. It's the equivalent of bench pressing 500 pounds on your first day at the gym when your left pec hasn't been working your whole life. It's not a great idea.

Dr. BJ Fogg's work on behavior design offers an excellent, practical mechanism of action for finding the right level of load. Dr. Fogg is the founder and director of Stanford's Behavior Design Lab, and he wrote the wildly popular book *Tiny Habits*. His behavior model is a simple equation:

$$B = MAP$$

Where *B* stands for behavior, *M* for motivation, *A* for ability, and *P* for prompt.[4] Let's unpack this. To inspire behavior, Fogg says we need three elements: motivation, ability, and a prompt. Motivation is how much or why you want to do something, ability is your capacity and skill set to actually do it, and a prompt is something in your environment that triggers the behavioral action. When all three come together, we create behavior.

Most people fail to change their behavior or form new habits, because one of these three elements is missing. Or it's there, but it's not at the right level to match the habit being formed. I'm a great example. When I told Bari how difficult it was to define my work, her answer—"Mastin, it's difficult because it's never been done before"—made me feel good. But it also shed light on an important context: it was hard because I didn't have the ability. Don't get me wrong, I had a generic level of ability. I'm good at what I do, and I could see the real change I was making in people's lives. But I didn't have the specific level of ability needed to do *this*, because no one had done it before. It *was* hard; it was new territory.

To build behavior, the intensity of these three factors needs to *match* the behavior you want to build. Take motivation as an example. Dr. Fogg talks about how in therapy and personal development, there's a major focus on motivation and you're told to always keep your confidence up. In that context, it's easy to blame yourself if you can't sustain that motivation. But you only need a sustained level of motivation to do difficult things. You don't need a lot of motivation to do easy things. People always talk about how long it takes to form a habit: 21 days, 30 days, 60 days, 6 months. But how long does it take to form a crack or chocolate or wine habit? Like, five seconds. Because it's easy to do. And there is a degree of emotional association. This lines up with Polyvagal Theory, which says you're more regulated when your system has the *right* degree of challenge, not too much. It took both Dr. Fogg's behavior model and Polyvagal Theory to finally convince me that I didn't need to make things so difficult for myself. Choosing the simpler route *wasn't* cheating. It was wise.

When I talked about this with my therapist, she told me something that shook my world. She said that many people who had trauma in their history were used to getting through some really difficult things. A big part of healing that trauma is realizing they don't have to anymore. It was like I had viewed the world in black and white my whole life, and now I was suddenly introduced to color. Those of us who have lived through trauma always assume we have to do things the hard way because we're oriented toward the most difficult path. Healing allows us to see that things can be easier, and it can mean a better life for us.

I often think about the entrepreneurs who broke through—the ones who achieved vast success and made a name for themselves. Almost all of them walked a difficult path. Elon Musk, for example, says that entrepreneurs need to be able to endure pain. And I love that because I think it's true. But it's only true for part of the journey. You can make things easier for you—and make it more possible for you to live in green—by spreading the load among a team. The analogy I always use is this: it's like I was walking into the gym, squatting with 2,000-pound weights, and then wondering why my knee was broken. And I didn't even think to look at the weight, because, to me, it was normal. Surely everyone squatted with 2,000-pound weights? But they didn't, and I didn't need to either. I just had to reach for a lighter weight.

Today, my focus is to make the things that matter easier. I design my environment to enable what I want to do and make it difficult to execute what I don't want to do. When I wake up, my exercise shoes are sitting right beside my bed, laces untied, the socks on hand. I put them on, leave my bedroom, and my treadmill is right there. It's a simple way to make sure I exercise every morning. Similarly, I keep a scale beside my mirror. This isn't advice for anyone else, but it works for me—the combination of the scale and a visual representation of my body works as a prompt to keep me in shape. If I didn't have a scale and mirror side by side, I wouldn't make progress. If I didn't have a treadmill that was super easy to get on, I wouldn't make progress.

Returning to our nervous system and Dr. Fogg's behavior model, when things are easier, you need less motivation. You also get more done because the challenge matches your ability. This is why it's vital to choose the right amount of challenge for your nervous system—just enough to knock you out of the green but leave you with the ability to build yourself back to the same level, making you stronger in the process.

We find the right level of stress through trial and error. We go slowly and see what does and doesn't work. Just like with strength training, it's equally important to focus on recovery. Sometimes problems arise not from being too stressed, but from being under-recovered. I had a client who was generating multiple six figures a year as a coach and felt exhausted; the solution to lessen their stress was to hire a virtual assistant. Another client added weekly hyperbaric chamber sessions and changed nothing else but saw results because they focused on recovery. One person adjusted their diet to less inflammatory foods and experienced improvement in their overall wellness.

The body gets stressed in many different ways—from relationships, workloads, environments, and foods—so we take care to assess the individual and understand where the greatest effect is possible. The best stress test is your own body. By building a better relationship with your body, you can notice signs of distress in your system sooner and take steps to get back to regulation.

We spend our time regulating emotions because we're doing things the hard way. People are always surprised when they realize they can achieve more by doing less. But you can. This is not to say that changes—even the simple ones—won't be hard, because change always is. But you can train yourself to see problems in a new light.

I coach many clients who want to move out of their full-time jobs and start a coaching business. Most of them are making $100,000 to $200,000 a year. Through our coaching program, they realize their coaching business will bring in around $400,000 to $500,000 comfortably. That's a huge profit. But then they start to panic. A bird in the hand is worth two in the bush, and they fear giving up the security of a job.

I ask them, "How long have you been thinking of making this switch?"

Let's say they reply, "Five years." Most clients say ten years, but let's keep it to five to make the math easy. If they make $200,000 a year in their full-time job and their coaching business brings in $400,000, that is already one million dollars they've lost. The point is this: People don't take action because they're afraid of loss. But when we help them put the loss in a different time zone, from past to future, they recognize that by not taking action there's an even bigger loss.

Change is hard. But the cost of not making change is worse. There is always a price, and most of us are paying it in passion, soul, and what we were born to do. It's fucking expensive.

Instead of avoiding change, find ways to make it easier. When you move from a full-time job to a coaching business, your nervous system will drop from ventral to sympathetic. It can't be helped. But you can titrate change by including other people in your process. Ask for help. When you open up and become vulnerable, you will be surprised by who steps up.

Finally, we must acknowledge that, within the patriarchy, there is more challenge for certain groups due to their skin color, gender, or sexual orientation. But there's still a way; there always is. A marginalized person can't model the journey of someone who is six feet, white, born in Kansas, and comes from the upper middle class. But they can look for people who faced similar challenges and still achieved success.

If you look for it, you'll find it. We're not trained to look for solutions. We're trained to be on defense rather than creating the life we want. This is especially true when we face an increased level of challenge. We spend so much time being stressed rather than doing the things that help us grow. But you can change that. You should. Because the cost of not changing is far higher than you imagine.

BEING PRODUCTIVE DOESN'T HAVE TO BE HARD

You can design challenge to be at the right level so that you can be more productive, by starting with your environment. Design your environment such that you make the habits you want easier to do and the habits you dislike harder. For example, I don't like to hit the snooze button, so I put my alarm out of reach and I keep the room cold. When the alarm rings, I have to get out of bed to turn it off and the cold wakes me up. I rarely get back into bed. Similarly, if you're trying to lose weight, don't keep sugary foods in your fridge. Eliminate the temptation.

Next, look at your people. Who supports you? Many of us lack reciprocity in our relationships: we give and keep giving, without getting anything back. Do an inventory. Does this person add to or take from your energy? Do you feel more or less inspired when you're around them? Make sure you have a support system that can give you good feedback.

Then look at your routine and shape it to make the behaviors you want easier. I have the same routine: I wake up around 3:30 A.M. and do all the intellectual work until about noon. My body is prepared with adrenaline and cortisol first thing in the morning, so I reserve that time for tasks that feel more complex for me. Post noon, as my system slows and calms, I can do what I'm wired to do: I coach people, write a book, or complete other enjoyable tasks that I can do with what I already know. Then I go to bed at the same time each night. Your routine doesn't have to look like mine, of course. I chose this routine because it aligns with my circadian rhythm. For a period of time, I was wearing a glucose monitor continuously. I realized I had this massive spike of glucose at around 3:30 A.M., so I went to my doctor, and he said that it was probably because my body was producing cortisol at that hour, which explains why I kept waking up. Now I get up at 3:30 A.M. and stay up. It's actually easier for me than waking up at 5 A.M. or 6 A.M., because it aligns with my body's rhythms.

Another way to reduce the level of challenge is with prompts. I keep a million prompts around the house to remind me to do things. I write them on big white tear-off sheets and post them on the walls until my office looks like a kindergarten nursery. One records my Daily Love first principles: *add value; be authentic; consistency, encouragement, self-love, community; six gives a week, one ask.* One note prompts me to reflect: *Whatever controls your focus controls your life. What am I focusing on?* Another is a reminder for patience: *Trust the dots will connect down the road. Little victories add up to a confident, decision-shaped destiny.* And one on business: *Deadlines have power. Embrace failure. Entropy is not on your side.*

But my favorite is the big white sheet where I wrote down the names and attributes of my parts. *Lil Guy: No one will show up and it won't work. The Medic: I disappear myself to rescue others. Han Solo: I'm the only one, and I'm triggered by competition. Professor Smart: I'm super smart, but incapable. Bomber: Fuck you, I don't need you.* I look at these notes all the time. When I'm brainstorming a new offering and thinking, *This will never work,* I look up at my note and realize that Lil Guy is speaking. These scrawled-on sheets are environmental cues to give my working memory an assist. Remember Dr. Fogg's behavioral equation, where behavior = motivation + ability + prompts.

Lastly, keep auditing your progress. Look for what you need to change to find the right level of challenge for you. Once you do, you'll find yourself growing in capacity and strength—and your dreams will be suddenly within reach.

PART III

HEALING YOUR RELATIONSHIP WITH YOURSELF (AND ALL YOUR PARTS)

CHAPTER 7

HOW TO LOVE YOURSELF THE TRAUMA-INFORMED WAY

"As long as you keep secrets and suppress information,
you are fundamentally at war with yourself. . . . The
critical issue is allowing yourself to know what you know."

— BESSEL VAN DER KOLK, M.D.

It frustrates me when people say "it's my trauma" and stop there. Yes, it's your trauma, but what are you going to do about it? Because if you don't do anything, the people who caused you the trauma win. It's not our fault that we have trauma. We didn't cause it. But it is our *responsibility* to work on it. Identification and acknowledgment of our pain is not the end goal, because that only leaves us stuck in our trauma response. Our purpose is to grow beyond it.

Several of these thoughts crystallized for me during my own therapy. My therapist—who is an absolute badass—is rooted in transactional analysis, which is a parts framework. According to transactional analysis, there are three ego states: the parent, the child, and the adult. There are two types of parent states: critical and nurturing. The nurturing parent state is comforting; it supports growth and self-expression. The critical parent state, on the other hand, is controlling and often demeaning. The famous language around the critical parent state is "impostor syndrome," for example; it is quick to label us. The child state also has two types: free and rebellious. The free child state is natural, easy, and a bit more compliant but also impulsive. The rebellious child state is just a perpetual 13-year-old who doesn't want to go along with anything, who keeps saying no, no matter what. The adult ego state exists by itself. In Polyvagal Theory, this would be our ventral mode, when our prefrontal cortex is online and able to make rational decisions. Think of this state as a chief executive officer who can absorb information from all the other parts (parent and child), analyze them, and then make a balanced choice.

Working with these three states in my own healing made me realize two things: First, most therapy stops at acknowledging your trauma; you learn about it, you understand it, but you never work on it. The missing key for healing? You know this already: *It's discovering your relationship to the trauma.* A big piece of trauma-informed care is helping people find their agency and choice, and you can unlock that agency when you explore your relationship to your pain and the parts of you that are hurting. It's basically asking yourself, "It's my trauma, *and* what am I going to do about it?" Second, the healing space has evolved to use trauma language that is based on the child state or the critical parent state. There is a lot of "you should do this" and then a reactive "no, fuck that," or a compliant acceptance of what is said. In this model, where the parent and child are elevated, the practitioner or therapist becomes the regulating force. The theory is that the practitioner is an externalized, healthy parental figure to whom you can go for a corrective, emotional experience to reparent yourself. Now, this model works. But it's also overly reliant on the practitioner, often to the point that when the practitioner disappears, the person falls apart. The key, I realized, is a focus on the adult ego state. I wanted to introduce a sense of ventral-vagal energy in attachment work so that my clients could develop their own self-energy or adult-ego state to stabilize their healing. Our aim was a ventral, adult state that was able to distinguish between "here's the trauma that happened to me" and "here is my response." Through this lens, we want to get to know our parts and *unblend* them so that we can recognize the reactions happening within us.

People come to me all the time and say, "Oh man, I'm so overwhelmed." But the truth is, they are not overwhelmed, only a part of them is. Which part is speaking? And do they have a good-enough relationship with that part to heal it?

This is the fundamental takeaway: improving your relationships with the different parts of you.

For example, if you say, "I'm procrastinating. What should I do?" Improve your relationship to the part of you that procrastinates. Or, if you say, "I'm suicidal. What should I do?" Improve your relationship to the part that's suicidal. When we approach our parts with curiosity to discover their purpose and intention, we create more connection, more understanding, and more awareness around what they're holding. It might seem crazy to think that a part that's suicidal has a positive intention; however, I've worked with many clients who've experienced such deep pain that parts of them have thought that ending their life would be the best painkiller. I myself have had suicidal ideation and have been to similar places in my own psyche. And while suicide doesn't end the pain (it only transfers the pain), it's understandable that any part that might be suicidal has a positive intention for the system to be out of pain.

We can understand intense parts, like suicidal parts, and recognize that understanding them does not equate to agreeing with their assessment of what we should do. However, the more each part of you can be understood, the more connection it will experience, and in the case of suicidal parts, it's not uncommon for them to recognize that connection and healing is a better choice than suicide once they're fully understood. My favorite thing to say to suicidal parts is something I learned from Dr. Frank Anderson, which is: "Welcome to the party, sweetie. I'm so happy you could join us. I'm so happy you feel safe enough to tell me how you really feel."

Ultimately, we want to improve. We want to change. Saying, "Here is my injury and this is my trauma response" is a good first step, but it doesn't help. You may be *smarter*, but you're still stuck. You want to take it a step further and say, "Yes, I was raped or neglected or abandoned. And because of that, here is my injury and the trauma response that happens unconsciously because of that injury. I'm starting to see the relationship between those two things. I'm going to work on bringing my adult ego or ventral-vagal state online so that it can be a moderator of this unconscious activity."

Trauma responses and triggers are best thought of as reflexes that our nervous system has learned over time to be the most efficient way to keep us safe. These reflexes are unconscious and out of awareness until we start to make what's implicit and unconscious explicit and conscious. By doing so, we can start to improve our relationship between the injury and the response (a.k.a. reflex). This is called neuroplasticity, and this is the work of healing.

I'm not arguing the individual becomes the ultimate regulating force, because coregulation is important. But the goal is to develop greater capacity, to be *with* the trauma instead of *in* it. For that, we need practitioners who point us back to ourselves to let this adult state emerge and connect with all parts of us and learn to love and accept them. Otherwise, they're the regulator—not us.

In our early years, we learn what is acceptable and unacceptable in order to maintain physical and emotional proximity to our caregivers, and we learn at a young age that if certain behaviors are unwelcome or cause disconnection, we start to fragment off aspects of our personality that can result in abandonment.

In my own life, one of the rules growing up in a house with a mother who had a broken back was to not do anything that would upset Mom or make her feel more pain. I learned at a young age that anger hurts my mom, or so I thought, so the ban extended to expressing anger. It wasn't until many years later I learned how to express my anger in a relationship in a safe and healthy way.

Ultimately, I want my clients to be able to sit with the parts that are unbearable and learn what is good and wise about them— and why they are valuable. I want them to realize that they can't be around certain parts of themselves not because they are rotten, but because their parents never could. That it makes sense they haven't developed relationships with these parts of themselves yet. But they can begin healing their relationships to each of the parts within themselves . . . and so can you.

UNDERSTANDING OUR INNER RELATIONSHIPS

A trigger is basically a piece of the past being remembered by the body. The less triggered we are, the more we are able to live in the present and move forward. When we move forward, we have ambivalence, a hot and cold inner conflict. Ambivalence exists because the past is alive, and it is doing its best to warn us about dangerous territory—and because the future is uncertain, it is always dangerous. Think of this "ambivalence" in terms of the laws of attraction and repulsion. Many people talk about the law of attraction, which is when you want something, you "desire" it. But as physics says, everything has an equal and opposite reaction, which means, as much as you want something, you are equally repelled by it. Say you want a loving and stable relationship. But the moment you enter into one, you fear it, because it's new and it has the potential to hurt you precisely because you care about it so much. So, you end up being resistant to it and push it away.

These laws of attraction and repulsion work for everything in our lives. Why do people procrastinate when they have to write a book? They don't procrastinate about watching Netflix or drinking wine. It's because those activities don't matter as much to them. Everyone has this inner conflict when they move toward what matters to them. This is why change is so hard. When we want to change something that's important to us, our resistance will be just as strong as our desire, because of the size of the change.

This goes back to our childhood. When we are young, we recruit the emotional and physical proximity of our parents to survive. It's just evolution—this is why mammalian youth are so cute. We learn quickly that certain behaviors recruit proximity from our parents while others repel them. This turns into rules of what we can and cannot do.

Eventually, we put parts of ourselves aside and don't self-activate, which means we don't look at our needs, desires, preferences, or boundaries. We suppress them. As John Bowlby says, "What cannot be communicated to the mother cannot be communicated to the self."[1] But it doesn't end there. Our adult goals then become reflections of this suppression. If I was bored and neglected as a child, it is natural for my goal emotions to be happy and nurtured. Our goals are intended to become corrective emotional experiences.

When something really matters to you, it's because you're starving for it. This part of you hasn't been fed your whole life. But it means the danger of chasing it is even greater, because your family won't approve. It is the one thing you could never say because then someone would hurt you.

Why do our goals and hopes and dreams bring us into inner conflict? Because they're trying to integrate the different parts of us, make us whole.

You see these dynamics play out across backgrounds. Think of someone who moved out of poverty and into wealth. Their whole family probably had rules about wealth and what rich people are like; they have had to break that generational trauma to achieve their dreams. I had a client once, an African American female, whose father was a pastor. When she and I worked together, we discovered a part of her that didn't want to be abundant because it felt like a betrayal to her father's struggles. Through dedicated work, she finally accepted that ultimate social activism is for marginalized communities to be financially empowered.

Remember that this internal conflict is entirely normal because multiplicity (of our selves) is a normal psychological phenomenon. I know you don't hear that often. When we think of multiple selves, most of us think of dissociative identity disorder. But multiplicity is a spectrum; dissociative identity disorder is simply one extreme. Anyone can have multiple emotions during the day. Just ask any entrepreneur or single mom. Every feeling we have, every thought, comes from different parts of us. We'll take a deeper look into how these parts are created and how to work with them in the next chapter. For now, just get curious about the community of people living inside you.

I think of multiplicity as our internal physics, with the same rule that everything has an equal and opposite reaction. For every trauma, there is a protective part that emerges. For every part that wants something, there is a protector to keep it suppressed. And there will be another part against that protector. It's a galaxy of parts, each orbiting around different things. Intrapsychic conflict occurs when there is a clash of opposing forces in the psyche. It's when we want something but also don't, such as the desire to be free that clashes with the desire not to be abandoned. This is what creates ambivalence. Each part of you has a different agenda, and it has to be effectively navigated for you to heal and integrate.

DEVELOPING A RELATIONSHIP WITH THE RESPONSE

Newton once said, "If I have seen further, it is by standing on the shoulders of giants." Viktor Frankl is certainly a giant. He came out of his horrifying experience in the Holocaust with formative and powerful distinctions about the human experience. His work has transformed how we understand ourselves. I often think of his quote, "Between stimulus and response, there is a space. In that space lies our power to choose our response. In our response lies our growth and our freedom."[2] Now, I'm not trying to explain something I've never experienced. I've never been in any type of adversity, let alone the darkness and trauma Frankl endured. But time has passed since Frankl made that observation, and we have more tools at our disposal, like Polyvagal Theory and fMRIs, as well as a keener understanding of the neuroscience behind our nervous system. To me, with that new knowledge, we understand now that the choice *doesn't* lie between stimulus and response. Our response is automatic because this is how our nervous system works. Instead, the choice exists in our *awareness* of that unconscious response. We can choose what we do with that response, and how we relate to it. This is an important distinction because so much of life coaching now is based on the idea that we can control our responses. It's the philosophy of "change your thoughts and change your life," which assumes a level of control that we don't actually have. This strategy may work for regulated people, whose prefrontal cortex is online and in control. But when we are in a trauma response or triggered, our prefrontal cortex turns off and we drop into the limbic system. We're responding immediately, automatically, without any awareness of why or what we are doing.

Remember alexithymia from Chapter 4—this inability to know what you're experiencing? It's normal and common. The key to healing and creating agency is to build interoceptive skills that help us understand what is happening in our body. We can then take the data we discover to our prefrontal cortex—that chief executive officer—and make a choice. So, with tremendous honor for Frankl's work and where it came from, I would say it is not stimulus → response. It is stimulus → response → awareness. Or, in the context of trauma specifically: injury → response → relationship.

When people with nervous system dysregulation or a trauma history go to life coaches, they are often told, "It's easy, just change your thinking," or "This is a limiting belief," or "It's a distortion of thinking." Those approaches ignore the nervous system, neuroception, and the body. They teach their clients to override their experiences or tell parts of themselves they aren't welcome, instead of working on creating relationships with their parts that ensure healthy data about their environments. It creates shame, guilt, and even victim-blaming.

I recently attended a life-coaching seminar where a client was suffering from cancer. The coach asked this woman a few questions and when they asked, "What are you feeling?" the woman said, "I am worried about dying."

"Well," the coach replied. "Everyone is afraid of dying."

The implied message is that the part of the client that fears death is not valid. It minimizes a very possible reality for her by ignoring her circumstances. Does everyone fear death? Sure. Is that fear larger and more looming when you are suffering from cancer? Of course. How can you tell the scared part of you that its fear is baseless?

Later in the evening, I watched this coach speak to another client, this time a woman of color. This client was talking about how hard it is for Black people to get clients. And this coach said, "You don't think it is hard for white people to get clients?" I was shocked. What privilege and lack of cultural context that question displayed. It ignored this client's genuine socioeconomic obstacles by telling her, "This part of you is not valid. Tuck it away." And this really is the problem I have with cognitive-centric approaches. In CBT (cognitive behavior therapy), a client could say, "My wife hates me," and the therapist will ask, "Is that real?" But what does that question mean—real for *whom*? Is it real to the client's prefrontal cortex? Maybe not. Is it real to the part of the client sitting with his therapist and discussing the nuance of hate and reality? Also, maybe not. But is it real for the part of him that feels that way? *Absolutely.*

Believing it is "false" creates an override or a suppression. Approaches that focus on the mind tell you that you can override thought patterns by creating new ones. And you can. You can create a new network with a new type of feeling. But if you ignore or negate the old network, it is not going anywhere—it will just get louder until you listen. And let me tell you, it will win. It is an emotional network that lives in the body, while the new network is cognitive; it is not as strong. Simply put, these approaches are unsustainable.

I know of someone who runs one of the most successful coaching certification companies based on a cognitive-centric modality. At a question-and-answer session, she was asked if her modality worked for anxiety. Her response? "I live with chronic anxiety, and this is the modality I use." You don't need to live with chronic anxiety! Chronic anxiety only continues if you are negating your nervous system response. If the person who created this famous cognitive coaching model can't get herself out of her anxiety using it, what hope is there for her clients?

PAST, PRESENT, FUTURE

So how does this model apply to the three states we talked about in Chapter 5: the past, present, and future? There is a lot of talk right now about neuroplasticity, which is your nervous system's ability to change. Neuroplasticity is influenced by learning and experience. When you experience something, your nervous system stores that data away to carry forward to future experiences. In other words, the past is always in play. Everyone has experiences that shape their nervous system. Everyone. So, whatever is manifesting for you in the present moment and keeping you from moving forward—because of course, past data believes that change is uncertain, dangerous, and a threat to survival—makes sense. All we need to do is figure out *how* it makes sense. This is what this whole chapter has been about: understanding the parts of yourself that have been shaped by the past and are now showing up in the present to affect how you move into the future.

Healing means nestling up to our past and making friends with it. It means being present in the moment so you can notice your somatic, cognitive, and emotional cues when they crop up—a tightness in your chest before a panic attack, a feeling of a boundary being crossed. Once those two things happen, you will spend less energy fighting with your past, thus giving you more resources to manifest creativity and imagination in the present and fuel your journey toward the future. And the better you understand your parts and can integrate them, the better people understand you. They learn how to support you so that you're not moving forward in isolation.

People fear this level of self-awareness. Nestling up to your past doesn't always sound like a great idea. And if we're present in the moment and consistently aware, doesn't that mean we hurt more? I think these observations are true. For a long time, I had the same concern. I would tell myself, *I don't have time to observe this. I have to work; I have to finish this seminar.* There were always better priorities. Until my body forced me to pay attention. When it brought me to my knees with pain in 2020, I tried to drown it with painkillers and yoga. I kept thinking, *I can't slow down, there has to be another way forward.* But there wasn't. I just had to stop and pay attention.

How difficult this process is depends on you. There are two questions I recommend asking yourself when you start this process:

1. How fast do I want to change?
2. Am I prepared for the speed I just chose?

So many clients tell me, "Mastin, I want fast change." But when they start to do the work, they become overwhelmed. They weren't ready. I'm not here to make the choice for you. Only you can decide at what pace you want to change, and how. But I can tell you that not changing will keep you stuck.

How many years do you want to walk around carrying the load and stress of not paying attention? Do you want to wait till your body brings you to your knees, as it did me? Or would you rather go through discomfort now for a better future?

In the next three chapters, we'll look at how to make change across our three timelines: past, present, and future. The start of any new behavior is uncomfortable. We cannot avoid that. But it's less uncomfortable than not making a change at all. For as Bessel van der Kolk said once at the Trauma Conference in Boston, "Before trauma work, your world seems small and isolated. But after you do the work, you realize you are stepping into a universe a lot bigger than you realized it could be."[3]

CHAPTER 8

HEAL YOUR PAST

"As long as you keep secrets and suppress information,
you are fundamentally at war with yourself. . . . The
critical issue is allowing yourself to know what you
know. That takes an enormous amount of courage."

— DR. BESSEL VAN DER KOLK

For a long time, I perfected the art of not paying attention. I don't mean my attention to people or businesses, but to myself. My focus was always to keep moving forward, no matter what, and that meant I was missing a lot of cues from my body about my decisions and relationships (which is where the crippling foot pain stemmed from). I didn't know it at the time, but a part of me was extremely neglected and alone. This part was rooted in my childhood, where I was pretty much left alone by my parents to figure things out. They had their own battles: my mom with her broken back and my dad pursuing his Ph.D. Even my birth was lonely; I was pulled out of my mother with forceps and then placed in an incubator for days, where no one could touch me and where my crying didn't bring anyone to help. It was a formative experience, with an imprint that lingers to this day. It created an incredible amount of anxiety and panic, and the only way I knew how to deal with it was to always be in control, always keep the power. It didn't help my relationships, and it certainly didn't help me.

Over the years, through challenges in my career and my body shutting down, I learned to build relationships with myself. I learned that this part of me, this neglected part, lives with a deep fear that no one will show up for him, and he will be perpetually alone. And I was proving that fear, day in and day out, by ignoring him. When I finally realized he was there, I made the little guy—that's what I call him—a promise that I would do my best to pay attention to him. And if I wasn't, I made him promise to let me know.

Now when the little guy stares at a book launch we're doing or a seminar or a talk, and he gets scared, my left ankle tweaks with pain. And I know he's basically saying, "No one is going to show up." So I say to him, "All right, buddy. You're right. No one is going to come. But guess what? I will be there. So let's go anyway." And we do, and of course people show up, and the little guy gets to see that the world is different from when he was created. We have a network now. We have people. By listening to him and giving him a seat at the table, I gave him a chance to draw new conclusions about the world. And the more I pay attention to him and the more he experiences the friendships I have, the less worried he is. Because he knows he will not crash and burn.

You know the most beautiful thing? Because I built a relationship with the little guy, the primary people in my life also know he exists. And sometimes when they know he is stressed or worried, they come to me and say, "Hey, let me talk to the little guy real quick." It is the most beautiful way to be loved.

TRAUMA (AND HEALING) IS RELATIONAL

I cannot repeat this enough: *trauma isn't something we get rid of.* We are not going to deny those experiences happened to you. Healing doesn't mean it should not exist in your psyche anymore. It means you have a better relationship to it. Why is this so important? Because all trauma is relational. Abuse is when someone does something to you and neglect is when they don't do something, but both involve other people. There are other versions of trauma, but they are also shaped by people: How did they respond or set you up to experience something?

Healing, therefore, is also relational. But it is not just with other people—it extends to the society living within you, that multiplicity of parts of yourself. Why does my little guy feel calmer today? Because I created a relationship with him. Because I said, "No matter who shows up or when, I will always be there." Each one of us has fragments of personalities and personas in us, created by formative experiences. Healing means becoming friends with those parts.

One of my clients was worried about people abandoning her as she formed friendships. We dug a little deeper into the feeling and realized that every time a person left her, she would reject the part of her that she believed caused them to leave. She worried she'd been too emotionally vulnerable, and that made her needy, so she rejected her vulnerability and neediness, thinking these were the reasons friends were leaving her. So, in fact, she was experiencing two abandonments: the friend leaving and then the part of her she was punishing for that leaving. Guess what? She would feel a lot less pain if she didn't exile the part of her that she thought was responsible for their leaving.

And that's the work we need to do if we want to heal: integrating and understanding the parts of ourselves. This is why we say the root cause isn't the trauma (i.e., what happened) or the injury response—it's the relationship to the response.

HOW PARTS ARE CREATED

In the last chapter, we explored the injury-response-relationship triangle and how healing may map across the three categories of past, present, and future. In this chapter, let's look at healing in the past—specifically, trauma and how it creates parts inside us.

Different modalities and coaching models speak about parts creation in different ways. As a Functional Life Coach™, I like to think of it as your history, similar to the history of the earth. Imagine a geologist on a trip to the Grand Canyon, or any place on Earth where you can see exposed layers of the land. Based on the soil, texture, and color of the layers they are observing, a geologist will be able to tell you this is where the Iron Age occurred or where the Ice Age happened. In other words, they are trained to read the earth's past. I imagine it is the same with us and parts. Every experience we've been through creates a filter through which we perceive the world and how we interpret its data: *Is the world safe or unsafe? Are people good or out to harm me? Is it okay for me to be myself, or do I have to be someone else?*

Imagine this process stemming all the way back to when we're born. We're consistently in feedback loops with the people and environment around us. This means that when we're younger, we are being programmed. When we encounter emotional pain as a child, our first impulse is often to express it. We scream, cry, throw tantrums. If the adults around us express discomfort or distress, or shut us down in those moments, our systems interpret their feedback as, "It's not safe to share this, no one can hold it. This will exile me from the group. I won't get Mom or Dad's love." And so we tuck away the pain and dissociate from it. In other words, we push it out of our awareness and into the unconscious. It becomes a layer in the earth of ourselves, a new lens through which we interpret the world, even though we are unaware of it.

Let's break this down with an example. When I was three or four years old, my father had to travel from Canada to Scotland for a work trip. To me, this was so far away. I believed he was not coming back. I was so convinced of this that I created an imaginary father factory in my head and believed I would have to go to the factory to choose a new dad. I was inconsolable. Then he came back from the trip, and I was genuinely shocked. Here was my dad, the same person—he made it home! My surprise was so memorable, my parents still like to tell this family story. But it shows that my little guy viewed that experience through the lens of "no one is there."

Life moved on. In adolescence I experienced my crush liking someone else—and I carried my wound and neglect into that rejection. *No one is there.* Fast-forward and I'm fired from my dream job. Now it's rejection and neglect, but amplified. *For real—NO ONE is there.* All these experiences shape how I interpret what happens to me. Anytime I uplevel, face uncertainty, or hit a roadblock,

Lil Guy speaks up. He says no one will show up for me and it won't work—which is why I wrote his refrain on a big white Post-it in my house, so when I hear those words, I remember it's him. No matter how much proof he has, this is his theme. If I'm not careful, he'll start to run the show.

When we tuck things away, they become unconscious. But they are still running the show.

Imagine all your tucked-away parts, shaped by your hurtful experiences, just slowly stacking up like layers in the earth's formation. How do we heal them? By going back to the earliest parts of us and befriending them. When I understand the earliest part of me believes no one is showing up, I can work on that. I can promise the little guy I will always be there. I can show him people do turn up. And once I do that, I can start viewing the world through a different lens.

Think of every science fiction or Marvel movie, where all these robots or aliens are waging war on the city. Fighting each drone is impossible, but once you take out the mothership, they stop working. Your original programming—the earliest part of you—is the mothership. The drones are all the other parts that arose in response to this programming.

Say there's a sad part of you that keeps speaking up, but you aren't getting what you need. So an angry part of you arrives that is upset you aren't getting what you need but that is also angry at the sad part. Then the critical part of you appears and tells you that you shouldn't be angry or sad. My point is parts create polarities. As we said in the last chapter, for every action there is an equal and opposite reaction—each part spawns other parts in response.

This work is not something we can do effectively on our own. Each of us has multiple parts that can speak up at once. We have blind spots and parts we haven't recognized. We can have multiple competing feelings, and thoughts about our feelings, and feelings about our thoughts. It's a mess that requires skilled help to untangle. I love to do this work with clients and have many programs that can support you in this process. But you can get curious: pay attention to all the different things you feel in a given experience, and be on the lookout for the parts of you who are speaking.

THE CEO OF YOUR INTERNAL BOARDROOM

Most approaches like neuro-linguistic programming and Internal Family Systems agree that every part of you has a positive intention. No one is out to harm you. Every part has a purpose. Conflict emerges because each part of you is trying to implement its purpose, without being fully aware of the other parts of you. It is like a loud, squabbling community where all the members can't really see each other, and everyone believes they know best. In fact, it's exactly like that. "A part is not just a temporary emotional state or a habitual thought pattern," says Dr. Richard Schwartz. "It's a discrete mental system that has an idiosyncratic range of emotion, style of expression, set of abilities, desires, and view of the world."[1] In other words, we each contain a society of people who are different ages and have different interests, talents, and temperaments. Parts of us can be enmeshed, blended, or operating independently. Some parts of us are rooted clearly in the past in connection to trauma, and when we're triggered, that part shows up to warn us of danger.

Loving yourself the trauma-informed way is understanding the positive intention of each part and helping them get along better. For that, you need a chief executive officer who can get everyone into a boardroom and say, "Okay, who is here today? Let's have a seat and take down everyone's perspectives." This is your adult ego state. This is you operating from your ventral state. This is you in green. To heal, the questions we need to be asking these parts are:

- What happened to you?

- How does it shape everything else that happened to you?

- Can we go back and reshape what originally happened so that you can experience everything else differently?

Without your internal CEO guiding this discussion, your parts are just going to fight more vociferously. But once they know there is a regulating force at play, they will eventually calm down. Because they know when they speak up, they will be heard.

If you want your life to be a roller coaster, just let your parts run the show at any given time. As you heal, you're going to discover different parts of yourself: frustrated parts, angry parts, sad parts, happy parts, parts that want you to go faster, parts that want you to go slower, parts that are exhausted, parts that feel like you're behind. We want to get all of them out in the open, and have your regulated self, your ventral-vagal state, lead and drive. It's like having a parent on the inside listen to all these parts like children, hear them out, understand them, and introduce them to each other, so they understand they're not isolated by themselves; they're part of a larger system.

As you've already read, you can't do this alone; you need a guide. In fact, the first thing I'd want to do with someone who told me they wanted to do this on their own is talk to the part that wants to do it on their own. It's an advanced skill set to be self-differentiated enough to listen to all your parts and to know your true identity is your heart, your soul, your spirit, and your regulated self, distinct from all your parts. Every one of us needs a guide to help us identify these deep elements in ourselves and practice listening with compassion.

Healing comes from understanding what your parts need and then giving it to them. Give them love, joy, safety, connection— whatever they are looking for. Move on from the theoretical conversation and just get them the nutrition they want. When you're thirsty, you don't take a chemistry class on how H_2O is formed—you just drink water. When you're hungry, you don't dive deep into blood sugar levels and insulin and leptin; you eat something. It's the same with your parts. Corrective emotional experiences will help them heal. And if you can heal the youngest parts of you that color all your experiences, if you can give them the nutrients they need, then the other parts relax, because the whole system is organized to protect the most vulnerable parts of you.

It's important to note that we aren't aiming to get rid of parts. We're simply trying to understand them better so that we have a

RECLAIM YOUR NERVOUS SYSTEM

clear idea of who's in the driver's seat. For example, shadow work is extremely popular currently. It's based on Carl Jung's belief that our shadow is the parts of us we suppress or reject, and it works to bring these suppressed aspects to our awareness. When people do this work, they have terrifying epiphanies. They realize there is a three-year-old making decisions in their business. Or a five-year-old driving their marriage. They now get to ask themselves, *Do I really want this part in the driver's seat?*

Healing internal conflict isn't about eliminating parts of yourself. It simply means building a relationship with those parts by sitting with them and understanding their intentions in a loving way. In Chapter 5, I talked about my ankle that was causing me agony for months. If you had told me then, "Mastin, this part of you has a positive intention," I would have laughed. I just wouldn't have believed it. But it did. It was trying to get me to pay attention—and it overcame every single painkiller I threw at it in sheer stubbornness until I acknowledged it. Only that acknowledgment could create healing.

If you take the perspective that every symptom is a part trying to get your attention, it changes your core assumptions. You will be able to move past "I'm overwhelmed/triggered/mad/frustrated/abandoned" to "What is this part trying to tell me? What is its purpose?" And that is so much more powerful than thinking, *How do I not be overwhelmed/triggered/mad/frustrated/abandoned?* because you are showing this part it is welcome. Suppressing does not work either, because it takes up an extraordinary amount of energy. I believe that chronic fatigue is just your body trying to repress emotions and running out of energy. It is exhausting to hold back emotion.

Yet it is also difficult to sit with our parts and talk to them. Why? Because in a patriarchal society, emotions are linked to the feminine and are suppressed. If you went downtown at one o'clock in the afternoon, with officegoers walking up and down the streets for lunch, and you let yourself act really excited—like, genuinely elated, screaming, jumping up and down—what do you think would happen? You'd be arrested. Public displays of emotion are allowed in certain circumstances—say there is a match on and your team wins—but otherwise, society views it as an aberration.

And that stitches in us a fear of emotion (a.k.a. affect phobia) from a young age. As French philosopher Blaise Pascal said, "All of humanity's problems stem from man's inability to sit quietly in a room alone."

We are petrified of our inner worlds.

Emotions and Our Bodies

When we begin work with clients, this fear is the first lock we pick. We remind them that it is only an emotion, and no one dies from expressing one. But lots of people die slowly from suppressing them.

Affective immunology is an emerging field of science that explores how emotional expression can change the quality of our immune system. In *Molecules of Emotion*, Candace Pert breaks down the science behind this: "My research has shown me that when emotions are expressed—which is to say that the biochemicals that are the substrate of emotion are flowing freely—all systems are united and made whole. When emotions are repressed, denied, not allowed to be whatever they may be, our network pathways get blocked, stopping the flow of the vital feel-good, unifying chemicals that run both our biology and our behavior."[2] We're just starting to understand the role of emotion in our bodies, but already the evidence is clear: they play a vital role.

One example of this effect playing out in our bodies is mystery pain: the kind of pain that shows up, stumps your healthcare team, resists diagnosis, and lingers unexplained. Common symptoms of trauma include:

- Back pain
- Stomach pain and digestive problems
- Feelings of weakness in individual body parts
- Feelings of heaviness in arms and legs
- Pain in muscles and joints
- Headaches and face pain
- Numbness or tingling in individual body parts

A 2022 study noted a "strong association" between these so-matic symptoms, trauma, and dissociation.[3] Research is finally starting to prove that blocking trauma out of your awareness can impact your mental and physical health. This is the process of so-matization, when your body expresses emotions you're unable or unwilling to feel. This is not to say physical disorders always have emotional roots. But when you somaticize emotions, you become susceptible to chronic illness. Your body will manifest what your mind has repressed.

TRANSPERSONAL THEMES

Here's a common pattern I see when people begin the work of ac-knowledging their trauma and the emotions their parts carry: they begin to search for meaning in their past experiences. These life lessons are called *transpersonal themes*. When I work with clients, we don't start looking for transpersonal themes until far along in the process, once we have looked at the nervous system, mecha-nisms of action, affected emotions, body sensations, what's going on in the brain, how we can create safe environments and develop relationships, and so on. The reason I open with this disclaimer is because if you rush into exploring your own transpersonal themes too quickly, you can override your nervous system and send mes-sages of invalidation. And that is something we never want to do. But when we can explore transpersonal themes without overrid-ing the experiences and parts that guide us there, this question of meaning is what usually helps them move to the next stage of growth.

Let's take my little guy again. What's his purpose? For me, his meaning is to show me we are better off in relationships that sup-port him. That's it. The whole fiasco is just so that I can learn to be in relationships that nurture all of me. But it's incredibly powerful to me, because I need that life lesson.

Now, it's important to remember that I'm not saying trauma is a "spiritual curriculum." In no way am I saying, "You chose your trauma," because you did not. But I am saying that if you have trauma, you have an opportunity to make it a spiritual curriculum . . . if you want to.

Every problem in your life has a primary and secondary benefit. I had a client once who would never leave the house. Staying holed up protected her feelings of stress around her personal agency and autonomy. But the secondary benefit was that her husband would drive her everywhere, and it gave her a sense of connection. Another client was struggling with rheumatoid arthritis. She had already done incredible work to heal and had come to me as a last-ditch effort. We were talking about her history at a retreat, and I said to her, "Do you realize your husband can love you when you're not sick?" Tears rushed down her face. Over time, as she experienced her husband loving her in her health, her outcomes significantly improved. Her transpersonal meaning was that she was learning how to be loved in her power, not her pain. And that creates a new context for any new challenges.

Jessica Mann, whose story I shared in Chapter 3, for example, has a transpersonal meaning of redefining what it means to be a survivor. She has been in the weeds of her trauma for a long time, so she didn't start there; she worked toward it. But now it gives her resilience and power, and she's used that power to put Harvey Weinstein behind bars.

People can find meaning and purpose in their trauma, and it can be a powerful way to recontextualize the worst experiences. But by no means do you have to if this feels uncomfortable.

CREATING CORRECTIVE EMOTIONAL EXPERIENCES

The simplest way to create a corrective emotional experience is to give yourself the opposite of what you did or did not receive. For me and my little guy, a corrective emotional experience is someone checking in on me and making sure I'm okay. For someone who was sexually abused, a corrective emotional experience would be drawing a boundary by saying no—and having that no respected. Let's put that scenario in concrete terms. Say a woman who was sexually abused is now in a relationship with a loving partner. This relationship is healthy, but she is still struggling with her trauma. A corrective emotional experience for her would be if the partner initiated sex, she said no, and the partner respected that no. Even better if the partner validated and celebrated that action by saying, "I'm so proud of you for drawing a boundary."

Corrective emotional experiences are deeply personal, and they vary from person to person. I had a client who was molested by one of her swim instructors, which gave her a deep phobia of pools. At one of our retreats, I asked her if she was ready to have a corrective emotional experience and she agreed. By some luck, we had managed to find a trauma-informed lifeguard who was female. We went to the pool, and the client got in slowly, at her own pace, knowing she could get out anytime. We then had the lifeguard hold her; she cried and released the fear that had been protecting her. The next day, she was doing cannonballs in the pool, after being afraid of water her whole life. Now, this may not have been the case for someone else. They may have needed a slower process and a greater range of corrective experiences before their trauma healed. It just depends—there is no right answer.

Another way to offer a corrective emotional experience is to complete something that was left incomplete. If someone was abused and was trying to push the person off them but failed, a corrective experience would be to push someone off or push a pillow off. It completes the action. It's also possible to rescript songs and places that remind you of your trauma. You can go back to a place of pain and make it a place of joy.

As one dark example, I think of several Nazi leaders who were hanged in Auschwitz. The place where they held all the power was now a place where they were powerless. It was a small corrective emotional experience for the survivors.

When I hold retreats, clients often describe their trauma, and when they do, their body slips back into the heaviness of the moment. They're crying, their shoulders are hunched, they are re-living the pain. I ask them, "How long do you think it will take for you to laugh about this?" Now, I want to be clear: My aim is not to make fun of anyone's trauma. We ask this question in a safe space, where the clients know they are supported and are in control. When I ask this question, most clients look at me like I'm crazy. Others are hesitant; they are not sure how to entertain the possibility of laughing about their pain. Still others say, "I don't know, in a week or two?" but you can tell they don't really believe it. They are just trying to give me the right answer—which they cannot, because there is no right answer. Then sometime during that retreat, we create an experience where they tell their story, but while they are in a different nervous system state—this time we choose a moment when they're in ventral (green). It's a strategy we borrowed from the world of Somatic Experiencing and the concept of pendulation, where you pendulate between trauma and play. They're telling the same story, but in a new state that we help them create. And I feel so much joy in seeing someone transform from telling a very heavy story about their trauma to legitimately laughing and having fun while speaking about it.

Part of my approach is to bring levity to trauma healing. Because trauma is already heavy enough, right? And if I treat my clients like they are fragile or only emphasize the gravity of the moment, they only relive the same emotions. But if I can inject play into someone's physiology of trauma, it helps them heal. This goes back to Chapter 4, where we talked about blending states to help us out of dorsal or sympathetic states. Introducing ventral regulation to a heavy experience can blend in another layer. It goes from only being heavy to being heavy *and* light.

And again, this isn't about making fun of your trauma—never. We are just giving your nervous system a wider range of responses to the event. Because ultimately, the way to help your parts—and heal your past—is to bring them out to talk and play.

The courses and programs that we offer will guide you here. This is the work I love to support people in. Corrective emotional experiences require exposure to emotions and experiences that were initially traumatizing. If you go into this territory on your own, you risk retraumatizing yourself. With skilled support, you can bring ventral presence to the journey.

CHAPTER 9

BEING PRESENT BY BEFRIENDING WHAT'S PRESENT

*"Neuroscience research shows the only way
we can change the way we feel is by becoming
aware of our inner experience and learning to
befriend what is going on inside of ourselves."*

— DR. BESSEL VAN DER KOLK, M.D.

In many ways, I "grew up" in the spiritual community—it's where I became sober and spent much of my 20s. The one thing they always tell you in spiritual talks is "be present." I've done a lot of vipassana retreats, spiritual retreats, and yoga courses, and everyone tells you to be present. Here's the thing: I had no clue what they were talking about. What did they mean "be present"? I was alive and breathing, wasn't I? Of course I was present! Where else would I be? But everywhere I looked, people were saying the same thing: "Be present." Coaches were talking about it, athletes, actors and actresses, even the brilliant Oprah, and here I was, baffled. Even those teachers who spoke about it in detail made it sound so complex. It was always about transcending ego and reaching enlightenment—a whole bunch of high-level concepts, but no way to actually do it. I was very clear: being present wasn't for me. For years, I clearly didn't get it. But when my therapist asked me to slow down, and I started to slowly and surely do the work with the geographical site of myself, I began to understand what all those spiritual teachers were saying.

Being present means being with the parts of me that are present.

In the previous two chapters, we've talked about how parts of ourselves are formed. When we experience an impactful event, a part of our psyche freezes at that age. When we encounter a similar sort of event or an event that we believe looks like the last one, this frozen part of our psyche reacts. So, when you're feeling triggered, *you're* not triggered. A 3-year-old part of you is triggered, or a 5-year-old part, or a 15-year-old part. None of those parts realizes it's *today*.

What do I mean by this? When a 5-year-old part of you is triggered, they react to your environment as if they are still 5. They face the problem that formed them with the same fears and anxiety as when you were young. But you're not 5. You're 27 or 32 or 45. And you are smarter now, better, more capable. Being present means telling that 5-year-old part of you that it is not the past anymore; it's *today*. And that means that while the problem looks the same, *you* are not the same. All the ways you've grown since then change how this new scenario will unfold.

But you can only stay present with your reality if you pay attention to the parts of you as they arise—no matter how uncomfortable or unbearable—and befriend them. If you want to stay present and in the moment, look to your nervous system.

HOW TO "BE PRESENT"

Think of the mechanism of action this kind of presence requires. Our prefrontal cortex must be online. Our sensory motor cortex, which is where our motor actions come from, needs to be healthy. Our limbic system needs to be downregulated to ventral, so we can breathe easily while being aware of our bodies and our environment. We steer clear of ruminating on the future or holding on to the past. We are here, and we are now. This is what it means to be present. This allows us to see clearly what's going on.

With these conditions met, when you are triggered by an event, you are able to be with the part of you that is awakened. You are able to listen and observe, with the potential to heal. Simply saying to that part, "I see, feel, and hear you," is immensely powerful, because this is precisely what your caregivers couldn't do. Not paying attention means you miss the emotional, somatic, and cognitive cues your body is giving you about the world, which leads to a crisis. Ask me and my left ankle.

Being present when times are good and we are in flow is easy. It's harder to pay attention when times are difficult, but this is precisely the skill set we need, so we must practice. We want to start by slowly exposing ourselves to the emotions we have a hard time feeling by using titration and pendulation (which we touched upon in Chapter 6). Here's what the process looks like: Trauma is multisensory, which means that when we are triggered, we occupy correlated body postures, breathing patterns, and emotional states. The first step is to breathe deeply. Breathing in oxygenates our blood, which helps our prefrontal cortex stay online, and breathing out stimulates our vagal nerve and regulates stress. The second step is resourcing. This is where we draw upon images and scenarios that give us strength. We may close our eyes and imagine ourselves in our safe place with our safe animal or safe person. This primes our nervous system for safety, because our brains cannot tell the difference between imagination and reality. Once we have primed our nervous system, we can step forward and explore the uncomfortable feeling triggered in us. This is a part of ourselves we need to befriend, but doing it all at once can be overwhelming—this is why steps one and two are important. Because the moment we feel overwhelmed, we can retreat to safety (created by resourcing) until we are ready to try again. This is pendulation, where we move from a dysregulated state to a regulated state, and back again. It exposes us to difficult emotions without allowing them to overwhelm us.

You may be thinking, *If we are closing our eyes and leaning into imaginary resources, how is this being present?* Think of presence as paying attention. Resourcing doesn't diminish our ability to pay attention and listen to what our body is telling us; it simply fuels us so that the process doesn't cripple us. Trauma work is difficult. We need anchors to guide us through it.

Orientation is another way to resource: you can look around the room for things you haven't noticed. My friend Adam and I go on walks and make a competition out of noticing things the other person didn't catch. You can orient internally by doing a body scan, checking in with each part of your body. Your imagination can conjure endless resources: When I first started my business and had no money, I would get on sales calls pretending to myself that I had a billion dollars in the bank. The brain doesn't know the difference between imagination and reality, which makes imagination a brilliant tool for creating a sense of safety in experiences that are novel and uncertain.

Here's a great question I learned from Dr. Frank Anderson that acts as a North Star for being present: Are you *in* this experience or are you *with* it? If you are *in* the experience, then your emotions have hijacked you. Your prefrontal cortex is not in control, and your amygdala is firing like crazy. You probably believe you are your emotions and body sensations. But when you are *with* an experience, you are able to observe it. You know it isn't who you are, but simply something you are going through. It's like you can hold it, outside of yourself. When you are *in* an experience, you are reliving a trauma state, but when you are *with* it, you are paying attention with a present state of mind.

REDECISION: A NEW NORMAL OF SAFE

Another good exercise when you are triggered is to ask yourself, *What nervous system state am I in: ventral, sympathetic, or dorsal? Green, yellow, or red?* Go back to the exercise we did in Chapter 4, where we looked at what the world feels like to us in each of those states and how we respond to our environment. Knowing these answers will help you notice your thoughts, feelings, and physical sensations without letting them run the show. It also opens you up to a great process known as "redecision."

Most of our development is formed in our earliest years. Based on our experiences as children, we decide (subconsciously, of course) what is safe or unsafe. When we progress into adulthood, we *repeat* those decisions in a process called "repetitive compulsion." So, if you've ever thought to yourself, *Why do I keep attracting the same guy in different shoes?* it's because you have a trauma that is trying to be healed. We just get stuck in loops.

Redecision is when we notice those loops and choose to break away from them. It's realizing it is not your fault you were abandoned or betrayed and deciding to opt out of the normalized childhood neglect by focusing on healthy relationships—in other words, swapping out the old conditioning for the new. Once we recognize we are in charge, we can reach for that new conditioning through daily training.

Redecision is powerful, but it cannot be rushed. A person must be truly ready to reconsider their boundaries, who they are, what is possible, and what they are willing to tolerate. Simply thinking *I choose differently* is not enough; it is not as simple as clicking "unsubscribe." Once you redecide and aim for that new conditioning, there is a process of realigning with the people in your life based on these healthier patterns. You will be able to find the people who elevate with you and form a healthy and supportive community. This is an important part of being present. So many codependent people, when they finally start taking charge of their journey, face the danger of becoming self-absorbed because they feel their earlier experiences were never about them and so now it is *all* about them. This is unsustainable. In healthy growth and relationships, you are open and receptive to your own emotions and body sensations, as well as that of others. You have the capacity to be with other people's emotions while maintaining your boundaries. In other words, your journey of healing is with other people. Being present acknowledges that and honors it.

But here's the thing about choosing new patterns: As you find your authentic self, you might expect the world to celebrate your decision. It won't. And when people disagree with the fuller self you're stepping into, it can be triggering. For example, a partner might interpret your change to your authentic self as you rewriting the rules of the game, and that can be threatening to them. So many people struggle when they get to this place in their healing, and they start once again repressing who they are.

We want to be receptive to our emotions, as well as the emotions of others—while holding on to ourselves, keeping our boundaries, and still having our needs met. It's possible, I promise. But it's hard to do. The good news? Being present makes it easier. Paying attention means you end this emotional fusion we often establish with people and realize that, "I am me and they are them; we are not the same." It sounds simple, but it is incredibly powerful. Because when you fuse, you're being someone you are not. You have to be—fusion isn't possible otherwise. "Two people becoming one" might be beautiful for a while, but not for a lifetime.

Remember, we are practiced at this emotional fusion because it is evolutionary. And there are appropriate stages for it. When the mother is carrying the child, this is a classic "two become one" moment. The body is flooding the mother with oxytocin as the pregnancy progresses, teaching her to identify the child as hers. Similarly, when the child is born, the child struggles to distinguish between themselves and the mother, for simple survival reasons. Remember, the mother is the first regulatory system for an infant. It's only when the toddler starts saying no that their sense of individualism comes into existence. And yet, throughout our childhood, we repress parts of ourselves again and again to achieve proximity to our caregivers, as we learn what is acceptable and what isn't. We put those "unacceptable" parts of ourselves away.

The process of redecision is bringing those parts back into play. This isn't just in the parent-child relationship. At the beginning of romantic relationships, both partners collapse parts of themselves to establish a union—and that is necessary. But then they stay collapsed and call this "marriage." A healthy relationship means differentiating between your partner and yourself while accepting you also have a relationship. It's acknowledging your shared reality while stepping away from emotional fusion. It's easier said than done because differentiation isn't modeled in our lives. This is why dysfunctional patterns can sometimes feel safe and healthy patterns dangerous. We become used to the trauma. Think of someone who is cheated on again and again. If it happens once or twice, it may be the circumstances or the other person, but if it keeps happening, then it's a pattern, and the person is part of it. There are cues in their system they keep missing.

Presence is how you break the cycle. What is your body telling you? What are your emotions saying? Focusing on how you feel in the moment helps you catch those warning signs. When we are not present, we ignore cues, which means we create allostatic load (i.e., the accumulation of stress). People come to me all the time and say, "Mastin, why am I burned out? How did I get here?" The simple answer is this: you missed the messages from your body for the last decade or so.

HOW TO SHIFT STATES

One of the most powerful tools to shift your state in the present moment is to have a baseline knowledge of yourself and the many parts of you, so you understand your triggers and what the different parts of you are saying. A few of the questions you can ask yourself on a regular basis to gain this understanding are:

- *What do I think and feel when I am in ventral, sympathetic, and dorsal?*
- *What are my behavior patterns when I am in ventral, sympathetic, or dorsal?*
- *How does my body feel in these states?*
- *Am I mostly in sympathetic, dorsal, or ventral?*
- *What are my triggers?*
- *Can I trace a trigger back to its origin?*
- *How did this trigger keep me safe in the past?*
- *If I let this trigger go, what are the dangers?*

These are questions that can help you form a good baseline understanding of yourself and how you operate. Cultivating a daily practice of sitting with yourself and checking in with your parts—asking, "Is there anyone in there who wants to talk to me right now?"—also helps establish dialogue.

Ultimately, the long-term well-being of your psyche depends on your environment: if your environment is not regulating, it is hard to be regulated. But there are strategies you can employ when you are triggered that can help you shift between states—say from sympathetic to ventral, or dorsal to sympathetic. Try the following tools to help you regulate when you are trying to shift states:

- **Create a space where you can calm down or cool off.** It could be a room in your house or a nice walk in your local park.

- **Breathe.** When I'm in the middle of an argument, I will often step back, take five minutes to breathe slowly, and then pick back up again. Peter Levine loves Voo meditation, where you say the syllable "Voo" out loud. This sound is common in Buddhist meditation, and Levine has observed clinically that it works to stimulate the vagus nerve to help create feelings of well-being and connection.[1]

- **Do a body scan.** Are you hungry? Do you need water? Taking care of your body's needs can soothe your nervous system.

- **Move.** Movement can help regulate and put you in touch with what you are feeling. The butterfly hug is excellent at activating your sensory motor cortex for regulation. In fact, any bilateral stimulation is great. You can shake it out, self-massage, or scan your body to release tension.

- **Check in with yourself.** What are your thoughts, feelings, physical sensations? Can you find the trigger and trace it back to its source? Do you know what part it has evoked, how old the part is, and how it thinks it is keeping you safe? Remember, this isn't an interrogation. Instead, think of this process as curiosity anchored in caring. If you do, you can eventually get to a place where you ask yourself, *I see how this reaction was helpful in the past, but do I need to be triggered in the same way right now?* It can calm you down.

- **When fighting with a spouse or partner, take space.** "Don't go to bed angry" is terrible advice. Absolutely go to bed angry, and then have the conversation in the morning when you are better regulated. Stepping away isn't avoidance; it's smart.

- **Set boundaries.** Telling someone, "I am at capacity right now and I need to stop this conversation," is powerful because it keeps the issue from spiraling and allows you both to revisit it when you are in a different nervous system state.

- **Share your experience.** One of the most regulating practices, especially if a person has been neglected as a child, is for them to share their internal experiences with someone in a safe way and allow themselves to be nourished by that person. The more you can set up the circumstances in your environment to support safety, the more nourishment you'll be able to take in.

VENTRAL GLIMMERS

Ventral glimmers is a term by Deb Dana,[2] and it's a beautiful way to guide yourself toward the ventral in daily life. Everyone has moments in the day when they feel really regulated. These can be micromoments—hearing a snippet of a song you love as you cross the street or seeing a bird in the sky—but they anchor you in a feeling of calm, relief, even joy. These are ventral glimmers: glimmers of when your nervous system lapses in the ventral state of happiness and possibility.

The practice of ventral glimmers is to focus on these moments— not to hold on to and unnecessarily prolong them, but to deepen your appreciation as they happen. It's about awareness. Because when you focus on the feeling, you bathe your body in beneficial biochemistry and you turn on your prefrontal cortex, which, as we know, is linked to the ventral state. In Deb Dana's words: "Sometimes simply navigating a day filled with responsibilities feels like an autonomic challenge. There are *glimmer days*, when noticing micromoments of ventral vagal energy can help you stay regulated and ready for connection. Other days feel more open, with time to pause and deepen into the longer experience of a glow."[3]

One of my glimmers comes from the ocean. I lived in Los Angeles for almost 15 years and took the ocean for granted. Then I moved to North Carolina for five years, to a mountain town, and I told myself I would never ignore the ocean again. So now that I'm back in Los Angeles, every time I glimpse the ocean, I pause for a second and say a silent thank you. It's a ventral glimmer, a little moment of joy.

The aim is to keep yourself open to these glimmers, so you realize when they happen. Think of it as a pathway into the ventral state from either the sympathetic or dorsal states. If you're chronically dorsal, it's hard to get to ventral without going through sympathetic, but moment to moment it's possible to go from dorsal to ventral. Cuddling, spooning, meditation, sleeping peacefully, having joyful sex—these are all blended dorsal-ventral states of being safe and immobilized. The more you notice these glimmers, the better you train your brain to find these moments of regulation and then stay in its biochemistry. Also look for opportunities to share these moments of beauty with someone, because sharing transforms the glimmer into an act of coregulation. It brings you out of isolation.

The beauty of these moments being short is that you feel no pressure to sustain them; there is no disappointment or shame if your attention wanders to something that isn't so relaxing five minutes later. The point is to recognize the moment for what it is and learn to let go. My friend Adam calls his ventral glimmers "BIDs" (Beauty in the Day). He tracks each one and writes them down. Sometimes, he'll come up to me and say, "Bro, two years ago on this day, my BID was you and here is what you said." It's a beautiful moment, because not only has he relived his moment of joy, but also he has given me a little ventral glimmer too.

PURPOSE AND THE PRESENT MOMENT

I've talked about purpose before and explained how it can guide our healing journey. But I want to take a closer look at it specifically through the lens of the present. We all come to the present moment from different places. Some of us arrive here from extreme trauma. Others venture here from a place of stress. Where you are coming from defines the context for that present moment, and what you have the capacity to handle. But ultimately, we want to ask ourselves, *What is this all for?* You are navigating your nervous system, speaking to your parts, and shaping a life that feels better regulated and healthier—but what is your goal for doing so? What is your raison d'être? When you can answer that question, the context of your behavior will change.

Most of us come to our healing journeys from a position of pain. Our context—the reason we so easily reach for—is often defensive and based around survival. *I want to feel better. I want to cope. I want to keep moving forward.* There is nothing wrong with these answers, especially at the beginning of your journey. But over time, if you can find proactive answers, your context will change from that of survival to productivity and motivation. You will no longer focus on just holding on. You'll be oriented toward thriving. For me, this is the missing piece in most trauma modalities around the world: They never ask you what your purpose is. But once you have a "why" behind your actions and behaviors, you have the rocket fuel for motivation.

Let's take a simple example. You wake up in the morning and look at the tasks for the day: It involves writing e-mails, planning meetings, and doing admin work. All boring things, right? But let's say you are doing all these things in service of a higher purpose: setting up a business. Suddenly these tasks seem less mundane: They are in service of a bigger goal. They are the tiny steps that will make your dream a reality. Knowing your "why" gives even the simplest tasks a different charge and energy. This applies to trauma work and being present in the moment.

So many of us, when we are triggered in the present moment, just want to avoid the feeling. We don't want to deal with it; we just want it to disappear. As you know from most of what I've been talking about in this book, wishing it away doesn't work. You need to be present, befriend the different parts of yourself, and work through the issues. *Purpose* helps you find the energy to do that. It gives you the motivation you need to not override or suppress what is happening to you, but to be with it and heal. If you are triggered in a situation and just want to hide, purpose helps you step forward and say, "Okay, but I made a decision to work through my childhood neglect, and addressing this trigger in this present moment is a step toward achieving that purpose." You recontextualize your healing work within a larger journey, which gives each step vitality and meaning.

Ultimately, purpose gives you agency and choice. It helps you see daily, in-the-moment work as steps toward a larger goal: "This is what it means to be an adult" or "This is what it means to choose a life of abundance" or "This is what it means to redecide." Attaching a "because" to your actions fuels motivation beyond just trying to feel better in this specific moment. Think of how many people change when they have a child. Suddenly, they now have a compelling purpose for what they do. They work harder or do better because they now think to themselves, *My child is watching,* or *I want better for my kid than I had.* It recontextualizes their behavior. A compelling purpose creates a compelling future.

THE CHALLENGE

All the data happens in the present moment. This is where everything takes place. This is how I think of it: You are in the present with the model of the past and desires for the future, and how you operate in this living moment determines how you can create a new future. To do that, you have to *be* in the present moment. You cannot rush through it like I used to. It turns out, all the spiritual leaders and motivational coaches were correct: being present is the key to unlocking a more abundant life.

Are you ready to start moving toward that life? To find out what's good about going slower and being present? This is the challenge I want you to commit to. Because if you breathe and focus on your body, pay attention to the parts of your life, and work on befriending the stress and pain, you can find your way toward a healthier, brighter future.

CHAPTER 10

MOVING FORWARD WITH PURPOSE

"Any sufficiently advanced technology
is indistinguishable from magic."

— ARTHUR C. CLARKE

One of my clients—let's call her Mary—was living on food stamps when she came to me. She had tried everything to make her business successful, but it just wasn't working. We sat down for an hour-and-a-half conversation, and she was deeply honest and raw about her past. Mary had been sexually abused as a child. Before she got into trauma work, she had unfortunately created a situation where her children were also abused—not by her, but by family members. She was carrying around an enormous amount of shame, both for what she had experienced and what her children had endured. When we delved a bit more into her childhood, we realized Mary's mom used to shelter homeless people from the street (a very Christian thing to do). These people were always kind to Mary and she felt safe with them, safer than she felt with the people from the church, because the people from the church were abusing her. Mary had linked homelessness with safety, and wealth and privilege with danger. Some part of her kept her living on food stamps, because that was pretty close to being homeless and thus where she would be protected. How did she move on from here?

Tony Robbins has this belief that I've always found to be true in my experience. In his seminars, he says people think you cannot change someone who doesn't want to change, but you can. You just need to find the right leverage.[1] Think of Charles Dickens's *A Christmas Carol*. Ebenezer Scrooge was not inclined to live his life any differently. But the ghosts of the past, present, and future created enough leverage to change his mind. This was the key: leverage. In his tremendous book *Man's Search for Meaning*, Viktor Frankl quotes Friedrich Nietzsche, who said, "He who has a *why* to live for can bear almost any *how*."[2] In other words, if you have the right motivation, you can find a way to move forward, even in the most difficult circumstances.

I have a lot of clients who come to me because they cannot act. There is always some reason: either they don't have the right data, or the elements haven't aligned as yet, or Mercury is in retrograde and so this isn't the right time. Here's what I tell them: Imagine you're in a theater and the long red curtain has caught on fire. You don't know the burn rate, the temperature of the fire, the material being burned, or how the fire started. Do you wait to gather this information? Do you tell yourself, "Mercury is in retrograde, so this isn't the right time to run?" Of course not. You just run. This is because the fire creates enough leverage to get you to move. It becomes what *The Talent Code* author Daniel Coyle calls the "primal cue."[3] Often, our primal cue is fear—this is what gets our attention and makes us act. But we don't always want pain to move, which is why we need a compelling reason.

For Mary to create the future she deserved, she had to find a compelling reason. Usually, we would focus on breaking the cycle of trauma so her children wouldn't experience the same pain, but her children had already been hurt. We needed to find new meaning and purpose. What finally got Mary to act was realizing that living in abundance was the only way to ensure her perpetrators didn't win. As long as she associated poverty with safety and wealth with danger, she was living her life in reaction to them. They had won: they kept her and her children down. This change in purpose shifted her behavior. She was able to unlock her potential and grow quickly from the brink of poverty to $50K a month. It was beautiful to watch.

I know Mary's example seems like a miracle. Poverty to $50K a month, just from finding a reason to change? Sounds incredulous. Like "magic." Which brings me to a quote from science fiction writer Arthur C. Clarke that I love: "Any sufficiently advanced technology is indistinguishable from magic." The power of this process looks like magic because we cannot distinguish what is going on. The truth is, Mary always had the tools she needed to achieve success. Most of us do. We live in an information age; none of us struggles with knowing how to do something. We struggle with implementing it—especially for Mary, where implementation would retraumatize her nervous system. Finding her purpose—"I don't want the perpetrators to win"—created a context change, and that enabled the "magic": a redecision to live a life of abundance. It helped her implement what she already knew how to do.

We're not experiencing cognitive challenges or a knowledge-base issue. Our barriers exist on a subcortical, somatic, nervous system level. Overcoming them requires finding a good-enough purpose to get off our asses, before a crisis hits. There has to be a better reason than a crisis to move.

GOAL SETTING AS A THERAPEUTIC PROCESS

Mary's story shows that goal setting doesn't have to be anxiety-ridden or traumatizing. In fact, it should be therapeutic and viewed as a corrective emotional experience. Most people create goals, re-create patterns from the past, and then think to themselves, *Oh, it didn't work again*. But if you approach goal setting correctly, with the right purpose and a compelling reason, it becomes a way to prove to your nervous system that something new is possible.

Purpose is your leverage. It elevates even the simplest of goals by contextualizing and organizing your behavior in a way that is incredibly powerful. I'll give you examples from my own life. One of my goals for the new year is to become a physical specimen at 10 percent body fat. The purpose behind this goal is twofold. First, I want to climb Mount Everest in a few years, and I cannot do that if I don't get in shape. Second, I want to learn to respect and trust my body again. The year 2020 was full of pain for me, and I lost trust in my body because it gave up on me. I want my faith back. Both of these reasons are more compelling to me than "I want to look good" or "I should be healthy." Tell me to do 10 push-ups because I should, and you're unlikely to see me move. Tell me to do 10 push-ups or I won't get to the top of Everest, and I'll suddenly have all the energy to get them done. Another goal of mine is to join several Masterminds. My compelling reason is simply that if I don't join, I will have less growth, less impact, and less community. The past couple of years in the pandemic have been isolating; we all know seeing people on Google Meet or Zoom isn't the same. It's been lonely. It's more motivating for me to think about Masterminds in terms of eradicating that loneliness than as a marketing or skill-set exercise. The same theory applies to any practical goal. For the new year, I've listed a revenue figure I'd like to hit. I've been stuck at the same level for so long, I've lost trust in myself, but hitting this figure will create that self-belief again.

Purpose differs from person to person, but it is always the leverage you need for your goals to become uplifting and achievable, as opposed to a loadstone around your neck. I work with a lot of mothers, and their purpose is often their kids. Kids learn more by imitating you than by listening to you, so my clients know that setting an example for their children matters. If they don't show up for their business and give it their all, they are teaching their child it is okay to slack off. But if they do show up, they give their kids an uplifting example of what it means to live fearlessly, with courage and bravery. And that motivates them to do it.

Once, when coaching in a group environment, I remember a man who would not commit to couples therapy with his wife. He just wouldn't do it, even though they obviously needed it. So, I went up to him, in the middle of the group—it was very dramatic—and whispered into his ear. He got furious and said, "Fine, I'll do it." You know what I said? I told him, "Bro, you need to go to couples therapy. Because if you don't, one day in the very near future, you're going to wake up and someone else will be fucking your wife." Now, that is not motivation that works for everyone—but it did for him, because the idea troubled him so much. This is what I mean when I say a compelling reason is highly personalized.

Don't seek out other people's ideas and motivations. Find what is uniquely important to you. If you do, you'll realize that the strategies we've discussed in this book for mental health and emotional regulation aren't just tools to feel better. They're supplemental; they support your purpose in the world. *How* to find your purpose is a juicy topic for a whole other book—and in fact, I wrote one for you called *Claim Your Power.*[4]

IMPLICIT VERSUS EXPLICIT MOTIVATIONS

Remember the story of my client who suffered from rheumatoid arthritis, who was learning that her husband could love her while she was healthy too? Now, she wasn't actively thinking to herself, *If I am ill, I am more lovable and cared for.* It was an unconscious thought, just like Mary's association of poverty with safety. We call these implicit ideas, concepts that are unconscious or unstated. Explicit ideas, on the other hand, are stated and conscious.

Every day, we work toward making our implicit thoughts explicit. We do it in relationships, at work, with family, and of course, in therapy. This is really the heart of it: taking what is unconscious and unstated and moving it into the realm of articulation and action.

You can identify a gap between someone's implicit and explicit goals based on the difference between what they say and what they do. It's easy to say "I want to lose weight," but if your behavior doesn't reflect this, then there is a mismatch between your explicit and implicit motivations. My goal is to help people have more congruence in their lives, which is when your explicit and implicit goals are aligned.

We need to start with the assumption that there are unconscious motives behind our behavior and that we do not know what they are. Functional Coaching™ helps you understand why you do what you do, why it is safer to do that action instead of what you explicitly state you want, and then how to make your explicit desires feel safer.

CONGRUENCE

When your implicit and explicit motivations align, you achieve congruence. In other words, congruence is when what you say and do is aligned with what you truly feel; it's the state we all should be working toward.

Congruence isn't the same as integrity. For example, you could be faithful to your spouse, which means you have integrity as a partner, but you can be incongruent because you don't want this marriage in the first place. Similarly, you can say, "I will never lie to my spouse about money" and if you uphold that value, you're living with integrity. But if you aren't expressing to them your desire to create more wealth as a couple, you're living with incongruence.

Congruence is most often aligned with authenticity, but to me it's a better term because there is less judgment associated with it. When you're congruent, you're able to surface your emotions and physical sensations to yourself and the people in your life. You're capable of acknowledging pain instead of suppressing it or looking an obstacle in the eye instead of ignoring it. It's when your stated experience or goals are in line with your inner experience—and that's the very definition of emotional, mental, and physical health.

It's a simple concept that is difficult to embody. I hadn't realized just how difficult it was until I became a coach. As a music manager, my job was straightforward. A client would call me, say they want to be on tour, and I'd get them on tour. They asked for something, I gave it to them, and everyone was happy. When I became a coach, people would say, "I want to lose weight," and then do nothing about it. I couldn't understand it. If they wanted something, like they said they did, why didn't they go get it? That question burned in me for many years before I realized we have trauma that is stopping us. We say one thing and do another because our actions keep us safe, but we also experience internal conflict and ambiguity precisely because what we say and do are at odds. Therapeutic models aim to get you congruent with the parts of you that you disowned in the past. The coaching process will help you become congruent today with the behavior that gives you what you want tomorrow. Functional Coaching™ aligns all three time zones.

WHY EMOTIONAL REGULATION STRATEGIES HELP YOU ACHIEVE PURPOSE

Here's a disclaimer about life that I wish everyone understood: *Going on a transformational journey will open Pandora's box of emotions.* This is because none of us are ready. I don't care if it's starting a new relationship, opening a business, having a baby, beginning your trauma-healing journey—whatever the next level of your life, you will not be prepared. You cannot be. Life doesn't work on the level of, "You're ready, so here you go." It says, "Here you go, now get ready."

That's important to remember, because every time you go on a journey toward a goal, there are several elements to it. The first is the external goal, which is what you are questing toward. It could be anything: becoming fit, pushing your business to new heights, healing your trauma. But achieving that goal is dependent on you mastering your internal state. The real achievement of every journey isn't the accomplishment of the external goal—it's who you become in the process. Who you *become* starts with who you are right now. Your emotions, thoughts, physical sensations, beliefs. And if you don't know what these are, then you're fucked.

There's a phrase I heard the other day that I love: "My gifts got me to a place my character can't sustain." Another way of phrasing that would be, "My gifts got me to a place my nervous system can't sustain." Because it's true: You start on this journey you've been longing for forever, and suddenly you're opening up different emotions, body sensations, and trauma—parts of you created at different times—that you have to tackle. And if you don't know how to handle that, and worse, don't know what's happening in your body, it can cripple you.

When I was in my 20s, I hadn't worked out for a year or two and then decided I wanted to be fit. CrossFit was all the rage then, so I went to a class, told them I had a poor fitness history, and asked to get started. They threw me into the deep end: running around the building for miles, pull-ups, push-ups. By the end of the workout, I was wrecked. I never went back there; it was too intense. A similar experience happens to people at the beginning of any transformational journey. They aren't prepared, and they get hit in the face with severe past emotions and barriers. If they don't have good regulation skills, they give up. They can't keep going because they don't have the tools to work through what's in their Pandora's box.

If we zoom out and look at this all together—purpose, self-regulation, and goals—then a simple way to think about it is: purpose is your reason, self-regulation is the skill set, and the goal is the outcome. Purpose gives power to self-regulation, as we saw in the earlier section called "Goal Setting as a Therapeutic Process," but self-regulation skills are what allow you to move toward and achieve the goal. You need to learn emotional, somatic, and cognitive regulation skills to achieve your purpose. Ultimately, purpose isn't a place or thing—it's an emotional state. It's what you live in most of the time. If you understand yourself and what you're scared of and why, you will have more agency or forward momentum to be able to be in that state of purpose. People refuse their calls to action (or what Joseph Campbell would name the "call to adventure" in the *Hero's Journey*) because it's simply too much. Not having these skills can stop you in your tracks.

SETTING GOALS

So how do you implement this information to set goals with a primal cue that motivates you to act? The first step is to interrogate where you are in your journey. In my experience, people are usually in three phases:

1. They are unaware their explicit behavior and implicit beliefs are incongruent.

2. They realize there is an incongruence between what they say and what they do, and they are making the choice to work on their childhood conditioning.

3. They begin to interrogate why their actions don't match their choices, and how to fix this.

Think of these three phases as denying, healing, and growing. Which phase are you in? Be honest. Understanding where you are in your journey helps you progress.

When it comes to setting goals that can uplift you and be therapeutic, the key is to find your motivation or primal cue. Ask yourself what gets you compassionately angry. Are there naysayers you want to prove wrong, or cycles you want to break, or missions you want to live? Do you have someone you want to prove right, or family you want to set an example for? Find what will get under your skin, that will push you to run like you're in a burning building. And if you don't know what that is, that's okay. This is why there are coaches and counselors to help you figure it out. But do it—take the time and the energy to find it.

Once you do and you have the fuel to achieve your goals, you can begin exploring the roadblocks to achieving them. How have you messed this up in the past, and how does that experience manifest when you reach for this goal? What can you do differently to make sure this experience is corrective, as opposed to traumatizing? Remember, don't go on the journey alone. From social baseline theory or Polyvagal Theory, the verdict is clear: People and community matter. Mountains look smaller when there is someone by your side. Get a coach, a group, a support system. Be wise about this support system: Choose people who know the road ahead and have traveled down it. Family and friends won't be any help if they haven't embodied the life you want. I love my father, but I wouldn't go to him for advice on how to start a business. If Richard Branson or Tim Ferriss was my father though, I would.

Lastly, make things easier for yourself. We've talked about BJ Fogg's *Tiny Habits* and how making large goals easier ensures they are sustainable. Apply that advice. Find relationships that help with your journey. If your environment is not working for you, change it. People come to me and say, "I live in a house where everyone is so negative. What should I do?" It's simple: Get out of that house. Epigenetics proves that the environment changes gene expression to a dramatic extent. You want your environment to match your vision board. Nothing will win over the environment in time.

PURPOSE IS EVERYTHING

Everything in our universe has a purpose. The purpose of the sun is to shine, a bottle to hold water, a tire to smooth our journey across roads, gravity to keep things in motion. It's the same with us. Each one of us was born with a purpose, and our task is to find that purpose. Because when we do, every aspect of our life aligns with our highest values. And this isn't only on a conceptual level—it manifests at the level of our bodies and our cells. The most evolved piece of machinery we possess is our prefrontal cortex, and it's loaded with the majority of our opioid receptors. The more evolved a creature is, the more receptor sites it has for emotion. You're wired for joy. This is why when your prefrontal cortex is online, you're in ventral and in a state of flow.

Ventral is connection and safety; it *is* purpose. When you understand purpose and bring your life into congruence, you break cycles. This is how you live a life that models the highest form of living for you and your family. This is how you get your best, most advanced machinery (your prefrontal cortex) to turn on. Inherent in your evolutionary design is purpose, and it is unique to you.

No matter how you look at this—through the body of research that proves the efficacy of purpose for everything in your life, through the lens of a Holocaust survivor who changed the therapy field, through the anecdotal evidence I've shared with you about clients—purpose is everything. There will be a day in the future when every doctor, psychiatrist, therapist, or coach will ask you the same first question. Not your weight or your height or your business goals or your emotional trauma. They'll ask, "Do you feel like you are living your purpose?" Because when the answer to that question is yes, your biomarkers improve. It's been proven.[5]

So, if you're looking for congruence and a better, brighter future, look for your purpose. It's the Miracle-Gro for the rest of your life.

PART IV

BEYOND TRAUMA

CHAPTER 11

BREAK FREE OF GENERATIONAL TRAUMA

"The effects of trauma can be transmitted to the offspring through mechanisms that are separate and distinct from genetics."

— RACHEL YEHUDA, PH.D.

One of the biggest but quietest obstacles to a person's success is intergenerational trauma. It's the elephant in the room we're only just beginning to notice, but acknowledging and working through it is key to reaching your potential. So, what is intergenerational trauma? According to Rachel Yehuda and Amy Lehrner, "On the simplest level, the concept of intergenerational trauma acknowledges that exposure to extremely adverse events impacts individuals to such a great extent that their offspring find themselves grappling with their parents' post-traumatic state."[1] Recent research suggests this isn't just passed down at the level of observed and mimicked behavior, but through nongenomic mechanisms that affect DNA functions. In other words, our parents' trauma affects how our genes express themselves.

To really understand this, let's look at epigenetics at the simplistic level. Your DNA is the most foundational building block in your body. Every part of you has DNA, so everything in your body is made up of the same thing, just *expressed* differently. This is why your nose becomes your nose and your ears shape into your ears—because your genes are told to express themselves differently in those areas. This is how an organism develops: genes at different sites of the body are told "you become a hand, you a foot, you a heart, you a brain" and so on. This is, of course, vital (imagine if you had lungs where your brain should be). But here is the interesting bit: not all of these instructions are following a blueprint; they're working on real-time data. You are made to be adaptable to your environment so you can survive, and you are constantly processing the data the world is giving you.

Your body is one giant biofeedback device.

Now, this doesn't mean your nose is suddenly going to develop into a hand. But epigenetics supports the idea that your environment fundamentally shapes you at a cellular level: it determines *how* your genes are expressed through a consistent feedback loop.

When parents have experienced trauma, neglect, or other adverse experiences and have not resolved it, it blends into their parenting and affects the development of their child. If your parents are extremely anxious, the gene for anxiety gets expressed in you. Experiencing anxiety once won't make an impact on your development, but if you are around anxiety all the time and thus feel constantly anxious, it becomes a personality trait. This is how trauma gets passed down from generation to generation: it dictates what genes get expressed, and that expression goes hand in hand with neuroplasticity. Both epigenetics and neuroplasticity are the building blocks of behavioral change. When we say, "The rich get richer and the poor get poorer," this is essentially a genetic expression remaining the same across generations. For the poor to get rich, you would need (among other things) epigenetic change. And for the rich to become poor, you'd need another type of epigenetic change.

How does this connect to our nervous system and the three states we've been talking about in this book (ventral, sympathetic, and dorsal)? The truth is, there aren't many studies that draw the connection; we're at the cutting edge of research right now. There are studies planned to discover these connections, but they aren't in the public domain yet. But, to me, our state affects our gene expression. The longer we stay in that state, the more drastic those changes become. Remember, states become traits over time. If you live in dorsal (red) or sympathetic (yellow) for long enough, neuroplasticity will rewire your neural pathways to make that state your default. You get locked into it, and it's harder to break out of. And because states interpret data from the environment in a certain way, your body is receiving certain types of data from the world that tells your genes how they should express. This is an oversimplification, of course, but the core message is clear: Our genes turn on and off based on the food we eat, the relationships we nurture, the environment around us, whether we're hydrated or nourished—all of it impacts epigenetic expression. Which, in turn, leads to the creation and sustenance of intergenerational trauma.

INTERGENERATIONAL TRAUMA AND MARGINALIZED COMMUNITIES

Rachel Yehuda is one of the most renowned professors of psychiatry and neuroscience and is a leader in traumatic stress studies, PTSD, and intergenerational trauma. In 2022, Yehuda and her team published a study on the impact of intergenerational trauma on minorities, specifically the impact of structural racism on the transmission of depression across generations.[2] It proves that our collective experiences as a group get passed down and, depending on who you are and where you are, they are passed down differently. Think of the historical trauma imposed through colonization, slavery, and displacement for communities such as African Americans, Australian Aboriginals, and First Nations peoples. This trauma is given to subsequent generations through environmental and social pathways, resulting in "an intergenerational cycle of trauma response, including physical (compromised immune system, endocrine impairment, and adrenal maladaptation), social (domestic violence, child maltreatment, substance abuse, involvement in crime) and psychological (depression, panic, anxiety disorders, post-traumatic stress disorder)."[3] For example,

Yehuda's study shows that depression among African Americans may affect children as early as in utero. Depressive episodes in mothers are linked to "premature delivery, low birth weight, and atypical adjustment"[4] in their children. This depression has been connected to structural racism—in other words, their environment treats them differently, and so different genes have been expressed in them.

Intergenerational trauma exists to a great degree among persecuted minorities; studies have traced similar cumulative trauma among children of Holocaust survivors. While not all of us have such heavy burdens to carry, the mechanisms that drive intergenerational trauma exist in all of us and manifest in different ways.

ACKNOWLEDGING YOUR INTERGENERATIONAL INHERITANCE

At its essence, intergenerational trauma tells us that what we've been through has been informed by what others have been through before us, because those genetic changes have been inherited. My father, for example, was a medic in the Vietnam War, and his acute gene expression passed down to me. One of the reasons I believe I have a compulsion to help people is because my father performed that role. As a fetus in my grandmother's womb, my mother had all the egg cells in her she would ever have in her lifetime. This means that the egg that made me was grown in my grandmother's womb. My grandmother was Eve du Pont, part of the wealthy du Pont family. They were businessmen and scientists, so in a way, I come by what I do very naturally.

In the trauma world, there are two sides: perpetrator and victim. My family are the perpetrators. All my life, I've felt a need to atone. I've felt it at a cellular level, but I never understood it. It's only when I started looking at intergenerational trauma and the history of my family that I realized that the du Ponts did a lot of good in the world, but they were also responsible for an immense amount of death. They were a significant part of the Manhattan Project, which created the atomic bomb that was later dropped on Hiroshima and Nagasaki. It ended World War II and helped the

Allies win, but the devastation those bombs created was unprecedented and unimaginable. Similarly, they supplied gunpowder during the French and Indian War and the American Civil War; it helped the North win and abolish slavery, but it also killed millions of people. Every good we did is tied up with some form of destruction. The American flag flying on the moon was made by a du Pont; we are responsible for creating Kevlar and saving millions of lives; we were very close with Thomas Jefferson and Benjamin Franklin in the early days of America, and we were intricately connected to the rise of this country. But the financial gain from that rise is complicated: It means we benefited from slavery and from pushing out indigenous people. We were in business with the Nazis until 1942, after World War II broke out.

I didn't have a chance to articulate or understand these reservations until I connected with one of my cousins, Lexi du Pont, in 2020. Until then, most people told me, "What are you talking about? You had nothing to do with those decisions. Look at the positive outcomes the family has created." And they have, and I'm proud of those positives. But there is a dark history there that sits in my nervous system, a history of elevating an economic agenda above ethical concerns. This is what my foot pain in 2020 showed me when I finally sat in the bathtub and listened to it: I didn't want to be just another du Pont making money. So much of my skill set comes naturally from them—they had the ability to understand scientific research and productize it. But their productization harmed people, and I didn't want to follow in their footsteps and traumatize the world.

I was only able to handle my intergenerational baggage when I identified it. Fear was holding me back: I feared walking down the same path they'd laid for me. It wasn't conscious; it lived in me at a cellular level. I only resolved it by talking to this part of myself that was forged before I was even born and showing it that I was focused on helping people heal trauma, not on creating more pain.

You already know how vital it is to see and accept all parts of yourself. Intergenerational trauma is the same concept but at scale. It's the ability to accept all parts of your inheritance: of your history, of your ancestors, and of your cultural context. For me, acknowledgment was a big piece: I knew my generational inheritance and its pitfalls, and I was committed to avoiding it. I have a picture in my office of Quan Yin, one of the most powerful spiritual avatars and goddesses out there, praying over an old-school du Pont book to cleanse it. It's a reminder, always, to purge my family karma.

Exploration into intergenerational trauma should be done with a skilled practitioner. But the following questions can serve as a starting point to get curious about your own inheritance:

- Are there specific traumatic events in your family's history, such as war, displacement, or persecution, that might still be affecting your family today?

- Do you notice any patterns of anxiety, depression, or specific phobias in your family that don't have a clear origin in your own life?

- How do the stories and experiences of your grandparents or parents resonate with your own feelings or behaviors?

- Are there any unexplained or unresolved traumas in your family's past that you might be unconsciously carrying?

- How do you react to stories or memories from your family's past? Are there strong emotional reactions or physical sensations that arise?

- Are there specific narratives or beliefs in your family that might be rooted in past traumas?

- How can you start a dialogue with older family members to better understand your family's history and its potential impact on you?

- What healing practices or therapies can you explore to address and heal from potential intergenerational traumas?

- How can you ensure that you don't pass on unresolved traumas to the next generation?

When we understand our relationship to our own trauma and our trauma responses, we can resolve our past and increase our internal regulation. Imagine if everyone had the tools to do this! And we do—they are built into each of us, because we are perfectly made.

HOW TO BE A TRANSITIONAL CHARACTER

Intergenerational trauma doesn't have to pass down from generation to generation. There are always people who break the cycle. This is why you see individuals who come from abject poverty for generations becoming multimillionaires—they've stepped beyond their generational trauma to create a new reality for themselves. These people are known as "transitional characters." The term *transitional character* was first introduced by Carlfred Broderick, an American psychologist, sociologist, and family therapist. According to Broderick:

> A transitional character is one who in a single generation changes the entire course of lineage. The change may be for good or evil, but the most noteworthy examples are those who grow up in an abusive, emotionally disruptive environment and who somehow find a way to metabolize the poison and refuse to pass it on to their children. They break the mold. They refute the observation that abused children become abused parents, that the children of alcoholics become alcoholic adults, and the sins of the father are revisited upon the children, to the third and fourth generations. Their contribution to humanity is to filter the destructiveness out of their own lineage so that the generations downstream will have a supportive foundation upon which to build productive lives.[5]

Each one of us can be a transitional character. Our intergenerational trauma is not our destiny: we can work through our history to emerge on the other side with new habits and ways of being.

To break free of the cycle, focus on being in a more regulated state, both with yourself and in the relationships in your life. Your cumulative and historical trauma is not your experience; it is the experience of your ancestors, and you have the choice to move away from it. Broderick talks specifically about breaking the cycle for your kids, but you can be childless and still be a transitional character because trauma affects everyone around you—your family, your friends, your co-workers. Trauma exists in multiple types of relationships. If you have done the work of breaking free of your generational shackles, then you can help people have a corrective emotional experience in relationships that aren't parent-child. It's just that simple. Resetting the foundation changes the game for everyone.

I remember once having a conversation with an African American woman about the racism she faced, and though I was trying to listen in service to her, I realized I was uncomfortable. I felt like as a white male I was the archetypal oppressor. My family had profited off the backs of slaves. That discomfort made it difficult for me to be fully present and to help. I talked to another leader about the incident and they said to me, "Until you can be ventral in these conversations, you have work to do." They were correct. Understanding where my discomfort came from helped me realize what my body was trying to draw attention to: that this was our history and there was a danger of perpetuating it. Explicitly acknowledging that history and reaffirming that I was going to do my best to not repeat the cycle pulled me into alignment with myself. I was better able to help clients from different backgrounds and be more congruent in my success. I know I have a lot of work to do. I have a huge amount of privilege, and my intention is to do good with it. For me, it comes down to the difference between chaos and alignment. Resolving my generational trauma makes me more aligned with the person I am and want to be, while unresolved generational trauma exists as chaos in my life. Resolved generational trauma helps me show up for my clients, not in a way that centers me in the conversation, but in a way that empowers them to achieve their own breakthroughs.

I love the advice that leader gave me because it hits the nail on the head. In most conversations about structural racism, white people show up with guilt, anxiety, and this belief that they are supposed to be the ones fixing things. If viewed through the lens of Polyvagal Theory, we would say they show up in sympathetic or dorsal. But all this does is reframe the conversation to focus on them and put a burden on the person of color who is sharing their experiences—either to figure out how to make the white person's guilt better or to assuage them. Showing up in ventral means you are prepared to work through your trauma on your own time. You don't place that burden on the person of color. It's also advice that applies to all situations. Struggling to have a conversation with your family about their behavior? Until you can be ventral in that conversation, you have work to do. It applies to every way in which generational trauma leaks into our lives. Our job is to do the work to feel calm and safe so that we can take on those challenging conversations.

Whatever generational pattern you inherited, those responses are part of a cycle. They are not a representation of you. This is one of the biggest revelations clients experience as they work on breaking their intergenerational trauma. One client in our program related that she'd been born into an environment of abuse, guilt, shame, rage, and resentment at the hands of her mother's alcoholic husband. In her 40s, this client learned she'd been the result of a secret affair, and the turmoil of this fact in her family had shaped how her nervous system was wired. As an adult, she repeated the cycles she'd seen and felt in childhood. She endured abusive relationships and marriages. She struggled to make moves toward her purpose, just like she watched her first-generation mom give up her purpose to take care of the children. This client was independent and intelligent and couldn't understand why she kept running into walls. She thought there was something terribly wrong with her.

But once she saw the pattern, she started to opt out of it. She realized she didn't have to be like her mom. She began to parent her son differently, because she realized she wanted to show him how to live in his purpose. When she began to date again, she stopped attracting addicts and alcoholics. Her self-talk became more compassionate: she realized she wasn't stupid; she was in a cycle that was separate from her true self, and she chose to break it.

I am constantly in awe of the parts of my clients that seem to want to grow no matter what they've been through. I've heard stories of horrible trauma, and yet somehow contained within each person is a desire to grow beyond past experiences into something different, new, and wonderful. It's an honor to be able to provide a safe space for not just healing, but for the creation of new patterns in people's lives. It can be so complex to honor where one has come from and the experiences they've been through, and yet on the other hand have a strong desire to create something new. I think it's so important to not make your history your identity. Nobody can control what happened in their past, but with a regulated nervous system and safe coregulation, an unlimited future is possible for anyone, no matter what they've been through. There's something about knowing that that gives me hope.

THE RIDE OF OUR LIVES

Bill Hicks, a comedian in the '90s, used to have this beautiful set about the world. He said it was just an amusement park ride, "and when you choose to go on it, you think it's real. That's how powerful our minds are."[6] It was big and thrilling—lights, noise, ups and downs, colors, glamour! In the end, it was a ride. But we forgot this. "Some people have been on the ride for a long time," Hicks explained, "and they begin to question: 'Is this real or is this just a ride?' And other people have remembered, and they come back to us and they say, 'Hey, don't worry, don't be afraid ever because this is just a ride.' And we kill those people."[7] It couldn't be just a ride! We had bank accounts, families, houses, worries. We'd invested so much in it, it had to be real.

But it *is* just a ride. It's not as scary as we think, not as weighted, not as petrifying. But it does take confronting things we aren't willing to look at. This is what it means to be a transitional character—confronting what most people aren't willing to look at, and then choosing to change for the better.

As Hicks concluded, each moment of our lives gives us a choice between fear and love. "The eyes of fear want you to put bigger locks on your door, buy guns, close yourself off. The eyes of love instead see all of us as one."[8]

This analogy describes all of us together in the world, but it also applies to yourself and all your parts. I think of human beings as fractals of the whole universe. There are voices of fear and love externally, but also internally. You have your own voices of fear that want to shut you up to keep you safe and protected because of what they've been through. But the truth is, you're most likely not in a traumatic experience now. While the *parts* that hold our experiences exist, the *trauma* you've been through no longer exists. Acknowledging that fact can be threatening to the system, because it would mean that the parts that hold the trauma for us could potentially be hurt again if we're not vigilant. Love can be scary because it makes us vulnerable. But when we recognize the trauma of the past is not in the present moment, and open ourselves to love, I think that's where a lot of healing can begin.

Choosing to let go can be risky to the system. But in the long run, it's likely riskier to keep re-creating the trauma. You can choose to create a different outcome than your trauma has led you to in the past. You can choose a different ride.

CHAPTER 12

HAPPILY EVER AFTER THE TRAUMA-INFORMED WAY

"We cannot solve problems at the same level of thinking that we were at when we created those problems."

— ALBERT EINSTEIN

I grew up watching *Star Trek: The Next Generation*. It was one of my favorite childhood staples. Every week, my parents and I would discuss what happened in the last episode and then we'd sit together to watch the next one. Captain Jean-Luc Picard, played by Patrick Stewart, was one of my role models: he would go into battle sometimes, but he was always a diplomat. In the Star Trek universe, beings not only have different-colored skin but also completely different body types. Characters are green, blue, brown, black, white, full-spectrum, and the differences between the different races and alien worlds are honored in Starfleet. The Vulcans are honored for their high level of logic, whereas the Betazoids are honored for their empathic and intuitive skills. It seems like everyone in the galaxy has gotten to the point where they disagree on matters of values and philosophy rather than needing to fight over the differences of the way their genes express in bodily form. Looking back now, it was such a gift to be given a vision of a universe where different types of people worked together in harmony.

In 1996, *Star Trek: First Contact* was released. It was about how the Vulcans made contact with the human race for the first time, because we'd achieved one of the criteria for being considered intelligent life: we'd cracked warp speed. I loved that movie when I first saw it as a 14-year-old, but I loved it even more when I watched it 12 years later, as an adult struggling through a life transformation. Because this time, I noticed that just before the Vulcans made contact, Earth had been pushed to the brink with World War III. It was the contact with aliens that united us, reminding us that despite differences of color, class, and nationality, we were ultimately human. And when we finally did encounter the Vulcans, we realized they too saw themselves as a unit, that they knew they were more similar than different. This is when I began to realize something: Technology in *Star Trek* wasn't just cool. It was created to even the playing field for everyone, to get rid of our basic problems so that we could live in harmony. No one in *Star Trek* is worried about money: they have food replicators to feed them, they have clothes, they are all treated with basic dignity. Gene Roddenberry had created a world in which equality, love, and diversity were the standard.

Star Trek and Roddenberry's storytelling has inspired so many of today's major players: Elon Musk was motivated to create SpaceX; Jeff Bezos was drawn to it. But for me, it was never the technology. It was the philosophy, that simple standard of love, diversity, and the interpersonal dynamics of harmony between races. *Star Trek's* utopian vision wasn't warp speed or being able to beam; it was that it had solved our basic problems of survival to push us past our petty differences. This is not even close to the world we live in today. And I'll be honest: This thought depresses me. I really believe there will be a time in our future when we look back on this—at the race differences, the class divide, the wars—and see it as the dark ages, the same way we now look at Genghis Khan's escapades across the plains or the Crusades. Just as we don't have polio or the plague anymore, we will evolve past racism and classism. We'll grow past our trauma patterns. I believe it.

But how do we work toward making this world a reality? How do we get closer to that gold standard *Star Trek* showed me as a kid?

The key lies in each one of us working through our trauma for a better life. Because once we do, many of our interpersonal conflicts will vanish; we can start moving forward into ventral and unlocking the potential of the human race.

An analogy that really brings this home for me is the cancer cell. Cancer cells evolve from our healthy cells; they begin by looking exactly like everything else and then, slowly, over time, they differentiate. But the intelligence of cancer is that it tricks the human immune system into believing it's still like everything else. It escapes notice. I believe trauma works in the same way. It's the underpinning of all our problems today. Being in trauma means we're defensive; we're approaching the world in sympathetic or dorsal and we're ready to fight or flee. Every war in the world means diplomacy has failed, and that means ventral has failed because diplomacy is ventral. World War II began because the German population had been ruined by World War I and the terms of the Treaty of Versailles. They were pushed into trauma and defensiveness, and when you're in that state, you will reach for anything to survive. This is why Fascism could rise and why Hitler could gain power. If you make anyone cold, tired, and hungry, they will be susceptible to manipulation. If people don't have what they need, they will do anything to get it. Trauma made the Fascists look like saviors. The Fascists, in turn, focused so intensely on their fear of the Jewish people that they brought about the very future they were working against. It was persecution of the Jews in Germany that caused Albert Einstein to flee to the United States—where physicists employed his equations to create the atomic bomb that sealed the outcome of World War II, and Germany's fate with it. This is a trauma loop at a worldwide scale.

Everything we're experiencing—classism, racism, lack of equality, lack of equity—it all arises from systemic trauma.

But the trick of trauma is we haven't noticed it yet. Not entirely. We still have trauma denial. And because we don't see it as a problem, it is slowly creeping up on us. It's shaping the world we find ourselves in. The only way to turn the tide is to change, one cancer cell at a time, back to health. To get our immune system to look up and say, "Hey, we have a problem here; this isn't good for the body." This is the value of each person embracing their potential as a transitional character: You support the healing of the whole one cell at a time. Diversity is necessary and beautiful, but ultimately, we are still one, occupying the same Earth and breathing the same oxygen. We cannot afford to lose our body, and we can only turn the tide when we acknowledge the cancer that's killing it.

Remember, the work you do has a ripple effect on the environment around you. And once you realize the impact your own regulation can have on creating a better world, we can begin creating a moonshot vision of a world free from trauma.

OUR PATH TO HEALING

If you look at the world from a polyvagal lens, it's clear we are moving from dorsal to sympathetic as a collective. For a long time, many of our issues weren't talked about. We shut down, swept it under the rug, declared it taboo, and refused to look at it. Classism, racism, sexism, lack of equity—these are all extensions of trauma that once existed outside the purview of articulated discourse. But now the world is sitting up and taking notice. It's demanding justice. Movements like #MeToo and Black Lives Matter are expressions of this shift from dorsal to sympathetic: they're shining a light on trauma and asking us to address it.

The anger that's arisen in all facets of the American population— the movements, the protests, the demand for justice—is a positive shift. To get from dorsal to ventral, you have to go through sympathetic; you have to get angry. At least now we're looking at the trauma; we're searching for how to create a more positive model for ourselves. But it's also messy. The one thing people always struggle with when they make the implicit explicit or speak their truth is that it isn't always met with joy and good vibes. You may have gone on a difficult journey to finally be your full self, but not everyone is going to be okay with it. And that's okay! Part of the journey is learning how to tolerate and manage the negative emotions of others, to understand how to properly place them. The point of discourse is learning to navigate differences. I see this tension among individuals all the time. A person will have finally found the courage to articulate what's been eating at them for ages; when they say it, they expect pomp and circumstance, but all they get is a hurt and angry partner who cannot understand why they would think that. Regulation means recognizing that this response is normal and is more about the person responding than the one speaking their truth. On the flip side, I tell my clients that it is imperative as partners to recognize the effort it has taken for the person to speak their truth. To realize what a big moment it is and why it is valuable.

These lessons can be expanded to the world at large. Take Black Lives Matter, for example. That was a difficult and powerful articulation of a truth that was kept implicit for a long time; it was a necessary discourse that opened society's eyes to how Black people are being treated. But many people responded with All Lives Matter, which is another way of saying, "I see your hurt, but I am hurt too," or "Why should I consider your hurt bigger than mine?" And of course all lives matter, but it was an unnecessary response. If you call 911 and say, "My house is on fire," they're going to send the fire truck to your house. Not to the closest house "because all houses matter." They'll send it to the one that needs help. In America, the Black community faces a different level of stress and dysregulation than the white community due to systemic racism. This is the truth. This doesn't mean that the white community doesn't have mental illness or poverty or doesn't suffer. It simply means when someone says, "Black Lives Matter," we have the option to respond with "Yes, they do" and really listen to that truth. It boils down to acknowledging someone else's experience without including yourself in the narrative. It means listening to your partner describe their hurt and saying, "I am so sorry that hurt you" instead of "Well, that hurt me too."

Right now, we're struggling as a society to acknowledge the experiences of different communities. And when people aren't acknowledged, they get angry. As Martin Luther King Jr. said, "A riot is the language of the unheard." I'm not endorsing riots or the destruction of property, but we have to understand where that behavior comes from. I've never met a rioter who has a full belly and a full purse and feels like they're being treated with respect. When the COVID-19 pandemic swept the U.S., businesses didn't riot when they received their Paycheck Protection Program funds. People didn't torch buildings when they cashed their stimulus checks. It's because people's needs were met. Typically, riots are a trauma response to an injustice.

Our country was founded on revolting against an oppressive government, so rioting is, in fact, a very American thing to do. But it is also a symptom, and if you want to stop the symptom, you have to look at the root cause: racism and lack of justice. Because if you keep blaming a dysregulated and marginalized group of people for being dysregulated and marginalized (and the behavior that comes with it) in a society that perpetuates that discrimination, you're never going to solve the problem. The one thing that riots show us is that our bodies will always try to get what they need, through whatever means possible. This is true at the level of the individual as well, not just communities.

I was talking to a client the other day who was describing a laundry list of all the things he had done wrong. He spoke about a rough divorce, losing access to his kids, partly running his business into the ground. And he was beating himself up for forming an unhealthy attachment to a woman during that time. I pointed out to him that it wasn't an unhealthy attachment; it was how he regulated during a trying period when he was processing a lot of grief. He needed that relationship at that point in his life. Recognizing that you're doing the best you can within your context is a vital step toward ventral regulation. Your system is always working toward getting what it needs.

I hope this book has shown you that your body is always acting in a way that's intentional; it's always trying to serve your best interests. You cannot vilify parts of you—that only serves to distance you from the parts that are trying to heal. You want a better life? You have to learn how to love yourself. Believe me, I hate that this is the answer. Love yourself? *Come on.* Every time I went to a yoga class and the teacher told me to "just breathe," every time I struggled with life and people said "slow down" or "live in the moment," some part of me screamed with frustration. It couldn't be that simple. It just couldn't. But, unfortunately, it is. It really is. Love yourself—all parts of you—and you'll be able to unlock your path to ventral regulation. It just isn't *easy*.

And that, truly, is the crux of it: it's simple but it certainly isn't easy. When my foot pain crippled me in 2020, I realized it was because I was ignoring my grief. Grief for the childhood I'd lost, for the things I wanted and never got, for the life I thought I would have. Today, whenever someone is volatile or impulsive, I've learned to ask them, "Are you grieving right now?" Because trauma work is linked to grief; we cannot escape it. Trauma, especially relational trauma, is full of missing aspects, and grief is the mourning of those aspects. It's the acknowledgment of the wound.

I hate grief. If I could edit the human genome so we didn't feel grief, I'd do it. Clearly, I hated it because all my problems—including debilitating pain—stemmed from trying to avoid it. But grief is like a master lesson; it comes with the territory. For new things to happen, the old has to change, and it's natural to grieve what is lost in that transformation.

I don't believe in asking, "What is the purpose of my trauma?" because it implies the trauma happened to you for a reason. It didn't. It just happened. But I do look to Viktor Frankl, who as I've mentioned created meaning from his trauma. When locked in Auschwitz, faced with the loss of his family and certain death, Frankl was able to imagine passing on what he'd learned to the world. He found purpose *from* the trauma of the Holocaust, rather than the purpose *of* the trauma of the Holocaust (prepositions matter).

The purpose I forged from my pain in 2020 was to make friends with grief. It helped me nestle up to parts of myself I'd disowned and turn on my creative brain and optimism. Today, I'm still on that journey. When parts of my body start to hurt or my environment feels off, I know I'm neglecting something and I get to work changing it.

But as I said, it's not easy. There are many layers to grief: grieving what happened, your needs that weren't met, what needs to be let go of, as well as the time you lost carrying this burden instead of acknowledging and healing it. It is not a pleasant process.

THE TRAUMATIC CINNAMON BUN ROLL

Here's the truth: Healing is the opposite of a cinnamon bun roll. We all love cinnamon bun rolls (or at least I do). It's the ultimate indulgence. You get hit with a craving, you buy one, you eat it, and boom!—it's amazing. Best thing you've ever tasted. You're on a high! You are pleased with your life decisions! Then you go to sleep, wake up the next day, and regret everything. The sugar rush is gone. You feel like shit. Trauma work is the opposite. You look at it and think to yourself, *I shouldn't do this, it's going to feel absolutely terrible.* And you would be 100 percent correct. It does feel like shit; you're starting with the sugar hangover. But then you keep going, you get to that reward, and it feels incredible. To bring green to the parts of you that were red and yellow makes your life more creative, playful, connected. You cannot wait to do it again. If the cycle of eating the cinnamon roll is desire → reward → pain, then doing trauma work and healing is pain → reward → desire.

So many people give up at the beginning of their trauma-healing journey because they're scared of the pain. Or they don't start (especially you, high achievers) because they believe trauma work will derail their A game. If only you could feel how your unprocessed emotions are creating drag on you. Once you clear them and get to orbit, it's easier to get to the moon. If you want to go far and fast with the same amount of energy, you must regulate. *You have to do the work.*

WHAT'S NEXT?

Albert Einstein said, "We cannot solve problems at the same level of thinking we were at when we created those problems." My hope is that this book has offered you a paradigm shift in your thinking. I hope you feel like your beliefs are being questioned and that you're both dissatisfied and joyful with how far you've come. I hope you commit to being a transitional character, to stop, break your cycles, and chase whatever is right for you. It could be starting a business, becoming a coach, being a parent, anything. But I hope you bring an awareness to it that gives you more self-compassion and compassion for others.

Because how you show up matters.

As a species, we haven't had the opportunity to heal our trauma—we've been too stuck in survival. This means you might be the first person in your family to do a lot of things, like go to college or be an entrepreneur. But if you're the first person in your family to break the cycle, you'll have made a large contribution to this world. Try to take it one step at a time. Look at the world from a nervous system lens, recognize when people are in dorsal or sympathetic, and identify the small moments when you are in ventral (green). Ask yourself: *What can I do to stay in a place of self-love and self-care in a ventral state? How do I find a community that shares my context around my goals and sees things as I see them?* Then you can take that foundation and channel it into whatever you define as your next step. Go create.

I hope this book has unlocked a creative impulse in you, because you've undergone a paradigm shift—you've understood life is a lot bigger than you thought it was, and the universe a lot kinder. Hold on to that impulse. Remake the world from that place of positivity and largess, from the beauty of being in ventral. If the lessons here have touched you, I urge you to share this book with your community so that you can create a shared context with them. Spread the word. If you're looking for the next step and guidance in your journey, hop on to mastinkipp.com to connect with me. I will be there.

I told you at the beginning of this book, in the words of the all-knowing Doc Brown from *Back to the Future*, that there are no roads where we are going. I meant it. But there can be people by your side, every step of the way, to help you find your happily ever after, the trauma-informed way.

In the words of Napoleon Hill in his classic *Think and Grow Rich*:

"'If we are related,' said the immortal Emerson, 'we shall meet.'"

In closing, may I borrow his thought, and say, "If we are related, we have, through these pages, met."

ENDNOTES

Read This First

1. My Frankl et al. "Psychometric Properties of the Affect Phobia Test," *Scandinavian Journal of Psychology* 57, no. 5 (October 2016): 482–8.

2. Frankl, "Psychometric Properties of the Affect Phobia Test."

Chapter 1

1. John Newport Langley, *The Autonomic Nervous System* (Cambridge: W. Heffner & Sons Ltd., 1921).

2. Stephen Porges, *The Polyvagal Theory: Neurophysiological Foundations of Emotions, Attachment, Communication, and Self-regulation* (New York: W.W. Norton, 2011).

3. Ruth Lanius et al., "Functional Connectivity of Dissociative Responses in Posttraumatic Stress Disorder: A Functional Magnetic Resonance Imaging Investigation," *Biological Psychiatry* 57, no. 8 (April 15, 2005): 873–84.

4. Porges, *The Polyvagal Theory.*

5. Thomas P. Blackburn, "Depressive Disorders: Treatment Failures and Poor Prognosis over the Last 50 Years," *Pharmacology Research and Perspectives* 7, no. 3 (2019).

6. Bessel van der Kolk, M.D., *The Body Keeps the Score: Brain, Mind, and Body in the Healing of Trauma* (New York: Penguin, 2014).

7. Todd M. Hillhouse and Joseph H. Porter, "A Brief History of the Development of Antidepressant Drugs: From Monoamines to Glutamate," *Experimental and Clinical Psychopharmacology* 23, no. 1 (February 1, 2015): 1–21.

8. John Elflein, "Percentage of People in the U.S. Who Suffered from Depression from 1990 to 2019," *Statista* (February 9, 2022).

9. Mary Dempsey, "Current Tuberculosis Statistics in the United States," *American Journal of Public Health* (March 1945).

10. Centers for Disease Control and Prevention, "Tuberculosis (TB) Incidence in the United States, 1953–2021" (July 8, 2022), https://www.cdc.gov/tb/statistics/tbcases.htm.

11. Garth Graham, "Why Your ZIP Code Matters More Than Your Genetic Code: Promoting Healthy Outcomes from Mother to Child," *Breastfeeding Medicine* 11 (October 2016): 396–7.

12. Jay Olshansky et al., "Differences in Life Expectancy Due to Race and Educational Differences Are Widening, and Many May Not Catch Up," *Health Affairs* 31, no. 8 (August 2012).

13. Kim Eckart, "Lesbian, Gay, and Bisexual Older Adults Suffer More Chronic Health Conditions Than Heterosexuals, Study Finds," UW News, August 24, 2017, https://www.washington.edu/news/2017/08/24/lesbian-gay-and -bisexual-older-adults-suffer-more-chronic-health-conditions-than -heterosexuals-study-finds/.

14. Rajeev Ramchand et al., "Suicidality Among Sexual Minority Adults: Gender, Age, and Race/Ethnicity Differences," *American Journal of Preventative Medicine* 62, no. 2 (November 8, 2021): 193–202.

15. Andrew Subica, "Cultural Trauma as a Fundamental Cause of Health Disparities," *Social Science & Medicine* 292 (January 2022).

16. Indian Health Service, "Disparities," Fact sheet, U.S. Department of Health and Human Services, October 2019. https://www.ihs.gov/newsroom/ factsheets/disparities/.

17. Rev. Martin Luther King Jr., "The Other America," Grosse Pointe High School, Grosse Pointe, Michigan. March 14, 1968, https://www.gphistorical .org/mlk/mlkspeech/.

18. SAMHSA's Trauma and Justice Strategic Initiative, "SAMHSA's Concept of Trauma and Guidance for a Trauma-Informed Approach," Substance Abuse and Mental Health Services Administration, July 2014, https://ncsacw.acf. hhs.gov/userfiles/files/SAMHSA_Trauma.pdf.

Chapter 2

1. Sigmund Freud, "Beyond the Pleasure Principle," 1920.

2. John Bowlby, *Attachment and Loss Volume One* (New York: Basic Books, 1969).

3. Substance Abuse and Mental Health Services Administration, "Trauma and Violence," September 27, 2022. https://www.samhsa.gov/trauma-violence.

4. Jeanne Supin, "The Long Shadow: Bruce Perry on the Lingering Effects of Childhood Trauma," *The Sun*, November 2016, https://www .thesunmagazine.org/issues/491/the-long-shadow.

5. "Trauma and the Brain." Posted by sdelboy. *Issuu*, July 20, 2018.

6. Tim Ferriss, interview with Dr. Gabor Maté, *The Tim Ferriss Show*, episode 298, June 4, 2018. https://tim.blog/2018/06/04/the-tim-ferriss-show -transcripts-dr-gabor-mate/.

7. John R. Pfeiffer, Leon Mutesa, and Monica Uddin, "Traumatic Stress Epigenetics," *Current Behavioral Neuroscience Reports* 5, no. 1 (March 2018): 81–93.

8. Bessel van der Kolk, "The Complexity of Adaptation to Trauma: Self-regulation, Stimulus Discrimination, and Characterological Development," in B. A. van der Kolk, A. C. McFarlane, and L. Weisaeth (Eds.), *Traumatic Stress* (New York: Guilford, 1996).

9. Van der Kolk, *The Body Keeps the Score*.

10. Frank Anderson, "IFS Introduction for Therapists Part 1," Therapy Wisdom, January 27, 2023, https://therapywisdom.com/2023/01/27/ifs-introduction-for-therapists-pt-1-frank-anderson/.

11. Philip T. Yanos, "The Impact of Illness Identity on Recovery from Severe Mental Illness," *American Journal of Psychiatric Rehabilitation* 13, no. 2 (April 1, 2011): 73–93.

12. Nagy A. Youssef et al., "The Effects of Trauma, with or without PTSD, on the Transgenerational DNA Methylation Alterations in Human Offsprings," *Brain Science* 8, no. 5 (May 2018): 83.

13. Ann E. Bigelow et al., "Longitudinal Relations among Maternal Depressive Symptoms, Maternal Mind-mindedness, and Infant Attachment Behavior," *Infant Behavior and Development* 51 (May 2018): 33–44.

14. Gabor Maté, *Scattered: How Attention Deficit Disorder Originates and What You Can Do About It* (New York: E. P. Dutton, 1999).

15. Brooke E. Poulsen and Joseph J. Coyne, "The Core Sensitivities: A Clinical Evolution of Masterson's Disorders of Self," *Psychotherapy and Counselling Journal of Australia* 5, no. 1 (August 1, 2017).

16. James F. Masterson, M.D., *Treatment of the Borderline Adolescent: A Developmental Approach* (New York: Wiley-Interscience, 1972).

Chapter 3

1. Dr. Joe Dispenza, *Breaking the Habit of Being Yourself: How to Lose Your Mind and Create a New One* (Carlsbad, CA: Hay House, Inc., 2012).

2. American Psychological Association, "Substance Use, Abuse, and Addiction," July 2022. https://www.apa.org/topics/substance-use-abuse-addiction.

3. Merriam-Webster, "Addiction," https://www.merriam-webster.com/dictionary/addiction.

4. American Psychological Association, "Regression." https://dictionary.apa.org/regression.

Chapter 4

1. Stephen Porges, "Orienting in a Defensive World: Mammalian Modifications of Our Evolutionary Heritage. A Polyvagal Theory," *Psychophysiology* 32, no. 4 (1995): 301–18.

2. Stephen Porges, "Polyvagal Theory: A Science of Safety," *Frontiers in Integrative Neuroscience* 16, no. 871227 (May 10, 2022).

3. Porges, "Polyvagal Theory: A Science of Safety."

4. Stephen Porges, "The Polyvagal Perspective," *Biological Psychology* 74, no. 2 (2007): 116–143.

5. Porges, "Polyvagal Theory: A Science of Safety."

6. Van der Kolk, *The Body Keeps the Score.*

7. Peter Payne, Peter A. Levine, and Mardi A. Crane-Godreau, "Somatic Experiencing: Using Interoception and Proprioception as Core Elements of Trauma Therapy," *Frontiers of Psychology* 6 (2015):93.

8. American Psychological Association, "Cognition and the Brain," September 2022, https://www.apa.org/topics/cognition-brain.

9. Roger Ekeberg Henriksen, Torbjorn Torsheim, and Frode Thuen, "Loneliness, Social Integration, and Consumption of Sugar-Containing Beverages: Testing the Social Baseline Theory," *PloS ONE* 9, no. 8 (2014).

10. Stephen Porges and Deb Dana, *Clinical Applications of the Polyvagal Theory: The Emergence of Polyvagal-Informed Therapies* (New York: W. W. Norton, 2018).

Chapter 5

1. "Neil deGrasse Tyson Teaches Scientific Thinking and Communication," MasterClass.com. 2019.

2. The Meadows, "Meadows Behavioral Healthcare Announces Deal with *New York Times* Bestselling Author Resmaa Menakem," Meadows Behavioral Healthcare, January 12, 2021, https://meadowsbh.com.

3. Patrick E. McKnight and Todd B. Kashdan, "Purpose in Life as a System That Creates and Sustains Health and Well-Being: An Integrative, Testable Theory," *Review of General Psychology* 13 (2009): 242–251.

4. Martin Seligman, *Learned Optimism: How to Change Your Mind and Your Life* (New York: Simon & Schuster, 1992).

Chapter 6

1. Victor Yalom and Marie-Helene Yalom, "Peter Levine on Somatic Experiencing," Psychotherapy.net. April 2010.

2. Scott Giacomucci, "The EMDR Resourcing Process Explained," Phoenix Center for Experiential Trauma Therapy. https://www.phoenixtraumacenter.com/wp-content/uploads/2019/07/EMDR-Resourcing-Explained.pdf.

3. Bessel van der Kolk et al., "A Randomized Controlled Study of Neurofeedback for Chronic PTSD," *PloS ONE* 11, no. 12 (December 16, 2016).

4. BJ Fogg, Ph.D., *Tiny Habits: The Small Changes That Change Everything* (Boston: Houghton Mifflin Harcourt, 2020).

Chapter 7

1. Mary S. Ainsworth and John Bowlby, "An Ethological Approach to Personality Development," *American Psychologist* 46, no. 4 (April 1991): 333–41.

2. Viktor E. Frankl, *Man's Search for Meaning* (Boston: Beacon Press, 1959).

3. Bessel van der Kolk, The Trauma Conference, Boston, MA, 2019.

Chapter 8

1. Richard C. Schwartz and Martha Sweezy, *Internal Family Systems Therapy* (New York: Guilford Press, 1997).

2. Candace B. Pert, Ph.D., *Molecules of Emotion* (New York: Simon & Schuster, 1999).

3. Leonhard Kratzer et al., "Co-occurrence of Severe PTSD, Somatic Symptoms, and Dissociation in a Large Sample of Childhood Trauma Inpatients: A Network Analysis," *European Archives of Psychiatry and Clinical Neuroscience* 272, no. 5 (August 2022): 897–908.

Chapter 9

1. Somatic Experiencing International, "Why the Voo Sound with Peter Levine of Somatic Experiencing®." Instagram, October 23, 2020.

2. Deb Dana, *Polyvagal Exercises for Safety and Connection: 50 Client-Centered Practices* (New York: W. W. Norton, 2020).

3. Dana, *Polyvagal Exercises for Safety and Connection.*

Chapter 10

1. Tony Robbins, *Unleash the Power Within*. Seminar.

2. Frankl, *Man's Search for Meaning.*

3. Daniel Coyle, *The Talent Code: Greatness Isn't Born. It's Grown. Here's How* (New York: Bantam, 2009).

4. Mastin Kipp, *Claim Your Power: A 40-Day Journey to Dissolve the Hidden Trauma That's Kept You Stuck and Finally Thrive in Your Life's Unique Purpose* (Carlsbad, CA: Hay House, Inc., 2017).

5. Samuele Zilioli et al. "Purpose in Life Predicts Allostatic Load Ten Years Later," *Journal of Psychosomatic Research* 79, no. 5 (November 2015): 451–7.

Chapter 11

1. Rachel Yehuda and Amy Lehrner, "Intergenerational Transmission of Trauma Effects: Putative Role of Epigenetic Mechanisms," *World Psychiatry* 17, no. 3 (October 2018): 243–57.

2. Sidney H. Hankerson et al., "The Intergenerational Impact of Structural Racism and Cumulative Trauma on Depression," *American Journal of Psychiatry* 179, no. 6 (June 2022): 434–40.

3. Hankerson et al. "The Intergenerational Impact of Structural Racism and Cumulative Trauma on Depression."

4. Hankerson et al. "The Intergenerational Impact of Structural Racism and Cumulative Trauma on Depression."

5. Carlfred Broderick, *Marriage and the Family* (New Jersey: Prentice-Hall, 1988).

6. Bill Hicks, *Revelations*, Dominion Theatre, London, 1993.

7. Hicks, *Revelations*.

8. Hicks, *Revelations*.

INDEX

ACKNOWLEDGMENTS

As this journey of words comes to a close, I extend my heartfelt gratitude to my cherished friends, family, partners, and to all who have been a part of my life's story. Your love, support, and invaluable contributions have not just enriched these pages, but have also shaped the essence of who I am. This book is not just a reflection of my thoughts and experiences, but also a testament to the wonderful impact you've had on my life. To all of you who mean the world to me, thank you for being my inspiration and my strength.

ABOUT THE AUTHOR

Mastin Kipp, a pioneering figure in personal development, established TheDailyLove.com, attracting millions. He is the author of two best-selling books, *Daily Love* and *Claim Your Power*, which pioneered the field of trauma-informed coaching. Kipp was the first to integrate Polyvagal Theory into coaching. Co-developing Functional Coaching™ with Jenna Hall, he transformed coaching. His podcast topped charts with more than 10 million downloads. Recognized alongside the Dalai Lama in *Watson's Magazine*'s 100 Most Spiritually Influential Living People and in Oprah's Super Soul 100, Kipp's selection for Oprah's *Super Soul Sunday* solidified his reputation as a leading thought leader for the next generation.

Reach Mastin at **mastinkipp.com** and **@mastinkipp** on all social media platforms.

Hay House Titles of Related Interest

YOU CAN HEAL YOUR LIFE, the movie,
starring Louise Hay & Friends
(available as an online streaming video)
www.hayhouse.com/louise-movie

THE SHIFT, the movie,
starring Dr. Wayne W. Dyer
(available as an online streaming video)
www.hayhouse.com/the-shift-movie

***

*CONNECTED FATES, SEPARATE DESTINIES: Using Family
Constellations Therapy to Recover from Inherited Stories
and Trauma,* by Marine Sélénée

*IT'S NOT YOUR FAULT: Why Childhood Trauma Shapes
You and How to Break Free,* by Alex Howard

TRAUMA: Healing Your Past to Find Freedom Now,
by Pedram Shojai, O.M.D., and Nick Polizzi

*YOU'RE GOING TO BE OKAY: 16 Lessons on
Healing after Trauma,* by Madeline Popelka

All of the above are available at your local bookstore,
or may be ordered by contacting Hay House (see next page).

***